THE BOOK OF DANIEL

ELIAS BRASIL DE SOUZA

Nampa, Idaho | www.pacificpress.com

Cover design resources from Lars Justinen

The author assumes full responsibility for the accuracy of all facts and quotations as cited in this book.

Additional copies of this book are available for purchase by calling toll-free 1-800-765-6955 or by visiting https://www.adventistbookcenter.com.

Library of Congress Cataloging-in-Publication Data

Names: Souza, Elias Brasil de, author.
Title: The Book of Daniel / Elias Brasil de Souza.
Description: Nampa, ID : Pacific Press Publishing Association, 2019.
Identifiers: LCCN 2019016092 (print) | LCCN 2019981341 (ebook) | ISBN 9780816365142 | ISBN 9780816365159 (ebook)
Subjects: LCSH: Bible. Daniel—Criticism, interpretation, etc.
Classification: LCC BS1555.52 .S68 2019 (print) | LCC BS1555.52 (ebook) | DDC 224/.506—dc23
LC record available at https://lccn.loc.gov/2019016092
LC ebook record available at https://lccn.loc.gov/2019981341

September 2019

Dedication

To Magela,

For her love, encouragement, and support

Table of Contents

Introduction

"Either do things worth the writing, or write things worth reading."[1] Exhibit A for Thomas Fuller's aphorism is the Bible's record of Daniel's life. He delivered on both counts. The book that bears his name and his steadfast allegiance are testaments to God's faithfulness, compelling all to listen and learn. Early Adventists were urged to study Bible prophecy: "Daniel and Revelation are the books applicable to us, and should be carefully studied, with much prayer."[2]

Historically, Daniel's authorship and date of composition have been a matter of fiery scholarly debate. Critical scholars contend that the book was written or compiled by an unknown Jew to comfort his people during the persecution inflicted by the Seleucid king Antiochus IV Epiphanes (ca. 167–164 B.C.). However, Seventh-day Adventists, along with other conservative scholars, view the book as being composed by Daniel himself in the sixth century B.C. They accept the book as an accurate account of the prophet's life and a reliable record of predictive prophecies.

Several arguments have been advanced in support of an early date for the book. Of first importance is the chronological information noted in the book itself (Daniel 1:1, 21; 2:1; 7:1; 8:1; 9:1, 2; 10:1). Second, some historical details recorded in the book show the author had firsthand knowledge of the historical events being recorded. Third, fragments of the book of Daniel among the Dead Sea Scrolls favor an early date. Fourth, the inclusion of Daniel in the Hebrew canon of Scripture also suggests an early date for its composition. Fifth, the Septuagint translation of Daniel shows that the book was already old by the second century B.C., since several words seem to have posed difficulties for the translators. Sixth, the matter seems to have been settled by Jesus, who referred to the book of Daniel as a composition of its namesake author (Matthew 24:15).[3]

One peculiar feature worth noting is that the book of Daniel (like Ezra) was written in two languages. Daniel 1:1–2:4a and 8:1–12:13 are written in Hebrew, while Daniel 2:4b–7:28 are in Aramaic. Most likely, this bilingualism functions as a deliberate rhetorical device to show different points of view, further reinforcing the message of the book. After a short introduction in Hebrew, Daniel proceeds to record his memoirs and two broad prophetic outlines in Aramaic (chaps. 2–7). Interestingly, these are the chapters that convey both Daniel's experience in Babylon and the prophecies related to the four world powers. Thus, these chapters were fittingly written in Aramaic, which was the international language of the time. But when the focus of the book turns to the sanctuary, the Messiah, and God's people (chaps. 8–12), the book appropriately switches back to Hebrew, the sacred language of Israel.[4]

The overarching theological theme conveyed by the book of Daniel is the sovereignty of God as the Lord of history, nations, and individuals. While the narratives about Daniel and his companions show God's love and care for the faithful exiles (chaps. 3, 6), the judgment of Nebuchadnezzar (chap. 4) and Belshazzar (chap. 5) reveals God's sovereignty in judging pagan rulers. The sweeping prophetic outlines of the book bring eschatology to the forefront of Daniel's message. In spite of the apparently accidental succession of kings and kingdoms, God will bring history to its consummation and establish an eternal kingdom under the rulership of the One designated as the Son of man, Prince, Messiah, and Michael (chaps. 2, 7, 9–12).

The present study divides itself into thirteen chapters. The first chapter addresses introductory issues relevant to the understanding of the book, such as its literary structure and basic principles of interpretation. The subsequent chapters follow the twelve chapters of Daniel, as found in the Hebrew canon and modern Bibles. As we engage in the study of this fascinating book, "let Daniel speak" and "present the truth as it is in Jesus."[5]

---

1. Thomas Fuller, comp., *Introductio ad Prudentiam; or, Directions, Counsels, and Cautions*, 3rd ed. (London: W. Innys, 1731), 40.

2. Ellen G. White, Letter 139, 1896, quoted in *Manuscript Releases*, vol. 18 (Silver Spring, MD: Ellen G. White Estate, 1990), 275.

3. Stephen R. Miller, *Daniel*, New American Commentary, vol. 18 (Nashville, TN: Broadman and Holman, 1994), 24–43.

4. See B. T. Arnold, "The Use of Aramaic in the Hebrew Bible: Another Look at Bilingualism in Ezra and Daniel," *Journal of Northwest Semitic Languages* 22, no. 2 (1996): 1–16.

5. Ellen G. White, "The Study of Revelation," *Pacific Union Recorder*, January 14, 1904.

CHAPTER 1

From Reading to Understanding

The book of Daniel begins in the ashes of exile and closes with the glory of the resurrection. One message rings forth throughout: God stands sovereign over the kingdoms of the world and watches over His people despite the evil powers that oppose Him and persecute His people. Kings and despots ascend to power and pass away, but in the end, the Prince of Peace obliterates the earthly powers and sets up a kingdom based on righteousness. Thus, no matter how complex certain portions of the book may be, one truth emerges loud and clear: Jesus wins.

Studying the book of Daniel is an exciting adventure, requiring a great deal of wisdom and understanding. Indeed, Daniel himself prays for understanding. His lack of understanding makes him feel faint and sick for a time. But an angel interpreter arrives to explain aspects of the divine message that require clarification. As you study the book of Daniel, you may feel like the prophet, longing for a better understanding of passages that seem difficult and obscure. In this regard, you may benefit from the scholarship of Adventist interpreters who have studied the book and explained its truths.[1] The present volume is a modest contribution to this end.

We will emphasize three elements to guide our study of this precious book. First, we will note its structure. The book has been organized along the lines of its narrative (chaps. 1–6) and prophetic sections (chaps. 7–12). Second, we will give attention to the proper approach to understanding the prophetic message of Daniel. Third, we will reflect on the contemporary relevance of the book of Daniel for our lives.

Structural and literary unity

As we study the book of Daniel (or any other biblical book, for that matter), we must bear in mind that God's special revelation has come to us through ancient modes of thinking and literary expressions. For example, we tend to present an argument in a straight line of thought: introduction, development, and conclusion. This Aristotelian-influenced line of reasoning, though foreign to the Bible, has become the foundation of the Western mind-set. To rightly understand the book of Daniel, it is important to set aside the expectation that its chapters and sections must unfold in a rigorous, straight-line manner.

In Daniel, we encounter a structure characterized by repetition and expansion, which applies to the prophetic and narrative sections. For example, literary parallelism is present in the lines of poetry found in Psalms but also functions in the large prophetic outlines and narratives in the book of Daniel. The prophetic outlines of Daniel 2, 7, 8, and 10–12 are a progressive chain of recapitulations and expansions. Each subsequent section repeats, expands, and adds information or details not previously covered. Likewise, the narratives are structured according to a pattern of repetition. The blazing furnace parallels the lions' den, and the temporary removal of Nebuchadnezzar from the throne parallels the permanent demise of Belshazzar. The outline below can help you visualize this structure:

- Prologue (1:1–21)
  - Four metal kingdoms (2:1–49)
    - God delivers Daniel's friends (3:1–30)
      - God humbles Nebuchadnezzar (4:1–37)
      - God humbles Belshazzar (5:1–31)
    - God delivers Daniel (6:1–28)

Four animal kingdoms (7:1–28)
The ram and the goat (8:1–27)
Daniel's prayer and God's answer (9:1–27)
The conflict of nations (10:1–12:4)
Epilogue (12:5–13)[2]

But the parallelism shown above by no means indicates mere repetition or circularity. In fact, such recapitulation must be qualified as a "progressive parallelism." That is, "the author takes us from the beginning to the end of a sequence of events and then returns to the beginning to describe them again, this time in different terms or from another perspective. One might liken the structure to a spiral staircase, turning around the same central point on more than one occasion, yet rising higher and higher at the same time."[3] As noted in every prophetic outline, repetition and expansion come with a historical progression that spans history from the time of the prophet to the establishment of God's kingdom.

It also bears noting that the narrative section (chaps. 1–6) contains prophecy (chap. 2), and the prophetic section contains narrative portions (chaps. 9, 10).[4] It is helpful to mention that the book begins in Hebrew (chaps. 1:1–2:4a), continues in Aramaic (chaps. 2:4b–7:28), and concludes in Hebrew (chaps. 8–12). A quick look at the literary and linguistic sections shows that they do not coincide but rather overlap each other, thus strengthening the unity of the book. Additionally, note that the Aramaic section (chaps. 2–7) is a concentric structure centered on chapters 4 and 5, emphasizing God's judgment on two rulers.

Another important aspect of the book that deserves attention concerns the interlocking nature of narrative passages with prophetic passages. The stories and prophecies recorded in the book should not be understood as independent strands that were later joined together.[5] Rather, the narrative and prophetic sections intertwine around each other in a tight unity. For example, the narrative notes about the seizing of the temple vessels by Nebuchadnezzar and their subsequent profanation by Belshazzar point to the arrogant activities of the little horn in chapters 7 and 8.[6] Likewise, Daniel and his friends' loyalty to God in the narrative section points to the faithfulness of God's end-time people in the prophetic section.

Interpretation of the prophetic message

Important to a proper interpretation of Daniel is the recognition that its prophetic message belongs to the so-called apocalyptic genre, which is a type of prophecy that stands in contrast to classical prophecy. Apocalyptic prophecies are of a revelatory nature, inasmuch as they disclose what has been hidden from human sight and knowledge; the prophetic messages preserved in books such as Isaiah, Amos, and Jeremiah are designated as classical prophecy. Apocalyptic prophecy also discloses God's long-range and unconditional plans for history, with a focus on the end of human history, pointing to a time when God will bring the present world order to a close and establish His eternal reign. Classical prophecy, however, focuses mainly on God's conditional plan for national Israel within the bounds of the covenant.[7]

Apocalyptic prophecy also displays other features. Revelation comes mainly in visions and dreams and often through the mediation of heavenly beings. It is also characterized by striking contrasts, such as good versus evil and the present versus the future. It may also use composite and vivid imagery—for example, winged lions and a horn with eyes and a mouth. All in all, apocalyptic prophecy emerges in times of crisis to convey a message of hope—God stands in control of history.[8]

At this point, we must remember that everyone brings an interpretative bias to the study of Daniel. Recognizing presuppositions and unique interpretational perspectives is the first step in gaining a proper understanding of its message. Throughout history, the prophecies of Daniel have been understood from at least four main perspectives: preterism, futurism, idealism, and historicism. Preterism views the prophetic events as already fulfilled. Futurism believes that the prophecies of Daniel will be fulfilled literally in an eschatological (end-time) period. Idealism understands the prophetic events as timeless truths with no specific historical referents. Historicism recognizes that the fulfillment of Daniel's prophecies takes place within the flow of history, from the time of Daniel to the establishment of God's kingdom.

To understand how these approaches differ, consider how preterism equates the antichrist with Antiochus IV. Futurism views the antichrist as a world ruler that will appear far into the future. For idealists, the antichrist represents any evil power that oppresses God's people or opposes the gospel. And historicists identify the antichrist with the papacy, whose power and influence extend from the Middle Ages to the end of the world.

Given these different approaches to Daniel, which one would be the most compatible with the nature and purpose of the book? Seventh-day Adventists have adopted the historicist view, not simply because of a supposed inherited tradition from the Reformers but because careful study has validated that the historicist view flows naturally from the book of Daniel itself. This fact is recognized by a reputable Adventist source:

> The validity of historicism as a method for the interpretation of Daniel and Revelation is provided by the fact that the angel interpreter in Daniel used this method in explaining the meaning of the visions to the prophet. In a dream he is informed that the dream of the king in Dan. 2 represents four kingdoms that will arise in human history before the kingdom of God is established (verses 36–45). The four beasts of Dan. 7 represent those same kingdoms, after which God will give the kingdom to the saints (verses 18, 19). The first kingdom was identified as Babylon (verses 36–38). In Dan. 8 two animals are used as symbols to represent the Medo-Persian and Greek empires (verses 19–21). The fourth kingdom is not identified in Daniel, but Jesus takes it to be Rome (Matt. 24:15). According to Daniel, this kingdom was to be divided, and a little horn would exercise political and religious control over the people. In the time of the end the horn is to be destroyed and God's kingdom established forever.[9]

In addition, Jesus understood Daniel 9:26, 27 from a historicist perspective as He referred to the future destruction of Jerusalem in A.D. 70 (Luke 21:20–22). And in the same vein, Paul mentioned a succession of prophetic events to be fulfilled within history before the second coming of Christ (2 Thessalonians 2:1–12).[10] From these observations, it follows that "historicism as a method of interpretation is found in the Bible itself, and it provides the key for the interpretation of the apocalyptic books of Daniel and Revelation."[11]

Let us turn to the year-day principle—a crucial interpretive element within the historicist approach. Three major reasons demand the application of the year-day principle to the time prophecies of Daniel. First, the magnitude of the events described in the prophecies leading up to the "time of the end" indicates that the time periods mentioned in these prophecies should extend through history and not be limited to a few literal days, weeks, or months. For example, from the broad scope of Daniel 7, it is unlikely that the struggle with the little horn would be resolved in three and a half literal years.[12]

Second, the symbolic imagery and language of the prophecy require that the time units be symbolic. As aptly noted, "In many apocalyptic prophecies, both the major entity and the time element involved have been zoomed down into a symbolic microcosmic scale that can be better understood by zooming them up into their macrocosmic fulfillment."[13] This has been called "miniature symbolization" and "allows the year-day principle to be applied to the 'seventy weeks' with their time subdivisions (9:24–27): 'a time, two times, and half a time' (7:25; 12:7); the 1,290 'days' (12:11); the 1,335 'days' (12:12); and the 2,300 'evenings and mornings' (8:14). But the absence of such symbolization in regard to the 'seven times' (4:16, 23, 25, 32), the 'seventy years' (9:2), and the 'three weeks' (10:2) implies that these time periods have to be understood literally."[14]

Third, the Bible presents ample evidence that a day can stand for a year. Numbers 14:34 and Ezekiel 4:6, as well as a host of other passages across the various books and literary genres of Scripture, reference parallels between a day and a year. Interestingly, the first time prophecy mentioned in the Bible seems to have been calibrated in terms of a year-day equivalence. Due to the corruption of the antediluvian world, God pronounced this verdict: "My Spirit shall not strive with man forever, for he is indeed flesh; yet his *days* shall be one hundred and twenty *years*" (Genesis 6:3; emphasis added). So the year-day equivalence that emerges in the time scales of apocalyptic prophecy already appears to be embedded in Scripture.

Contemporary relevance

To understand the book of Daniel, we must know more than the history and dates related to its prophecies; we must read it to learn about the God who revealed Himself in its narratives and prophecies. On every page, God shows Himself to be in control. At the beginning of the book, He gives Jerusalem over to Nebuchadnezzar, but at the end, He raises His people from the dead. As the book unfolds, God watches over His servants and gives them wisdom. He accompanies them in the blazing furnace and the den of lions. He sets up kings and removes them, revealing His long-range plan to establish His eternal kingdom.

The book of Daniel bears witness to Christ by disclosing God's grace and highlighting its ultimate revelation in Jesus. The merciful nature of God and what He does for His people point to Jesus as Savior and Lord. The fourth Man in the blazing furnace and the Man clothed in linen are specific disclosures of the preincarnate Christ. But Christ also appears at the heart of the prophetic message of the book as our Sacrifice, Priest, and King.

The lordship of Christ is also evident in the narratives of Daniel and his friends, providing models of excellence, integrity, and wisdom. They inspire us to live faithful lives as we serve God in a pluralistic and relativistic culture. Ellen White notes, "A faithful study of the story of Daniel and his three friends will teach the principles that underlie a strong, true character. These young men had first learned to serve God in their homes. They had there learned the meaning of true religion and what God would do for them if they remained loyal to him. When they were carried to the court of Babylon, they determined to yield up life itself rather than be untrue to God."[15] As one writer has asserted, "There is not a square inch in the whole domain of our human existence over which Christ, who is Sovereign over *all*, does not cry: 'Mine!' "[16]

The book of Daniel also aids us in understanding the biblical worldview. Its portrayal of God, for example, provides glimpses into the nature of ultimate reality. God communicates with humans, predicts the future, and drives history forward to its consummation. This view of ultimate reality stands in sharp contrast to pantheism, deism, and materialism. Amid the many competing approaches to life, the book of Daniel serves as a spiritual GPS, orienting us to our current position and our ultimate destination in God's plan.

Finally, the book of Daniel highlights the privilege and responsibility of the remnant people. One historian's comment on a specific verse can certainly apply to the book as a whole: "Daniel 8:14 is not so much for personal salvation as it is an anchor point in time for a final world mission that would take a special message to every nation, tribe, and tongue (Revelation 10:11; 14:6)."[17] To a large extent, our identity, message, and mission are grounded in the prophetic message of Daniel.

Conclusion

This information can help us to navigate the book of Daniel. As we journey through its pages, we will encounter a landscape populated with various creatures. We will meet prayerful people, arrogant kings, hybrid animals, speaking horns, and brilliant angels. But above every character and every prophecy stands the all-powerful Sovereign of the universe. It is He who drives the flow of history to its ultimate goal. We will find Him walking in a fiery furnace, moving in a den of lions, serving in the heavenly court, or even standing above a river. But in the end, we will meet Michael, our Prince, face-to-face—the One who abides with us in life and death!

---

1. See, e.g., Frank B. Holbrook, ed., *Symposium on Daniel*, vol. 2, Daniel and Revelation Committee Series (Washington, DC: Biblical Research Institute,

1986); Gerhard Pfandl, *Daniel: The Seer of Babylon* (Hagerstown, MD: Review and Herald®, 2004); William H. Shea, *Daniel: A Reader's Guide* (Nampa, ID: Pacific Press®, 2005).

2. Adapted from Mitchell Loyd Chase, "Resurrection Hope in Daniel 12:2: An Exercise in Biblical Theology" (PhD diss., Southern Baptist Theological Seminary, 2013), 48; Peter J. Gentry and Stephen J. Wellum, *Kingdom Through Covenant: A Biblical-Theological Understanding of the Covenants* (Wheaton, IL: Crossway, 2012), 531, 532; Andrew E. Steinmann, *Daniel*, Concordia Commentary (St. Louis, MO: Concordia, 2008), 22, 23.

3. Sinclair B. Ferguson, *Daniel*, Preacher's Commentary, vol. 21 (Nashville, TN: Thomas Nelson, 1988), 17.

4. Carol A. Newsom and Brennan W. Breed, *Daniel: A Commentary*, Old Testament Library (Louisville, KY: Westminster John Knox, 2014), 289.

5. John J. Collins, *Daniel: A Commentary on the Book of Daniel*, Hermeneia (Minneapolis, MN: Fortress, 1994), 37–39.

6. Winfried Vogel, "Cultic Motifs and Themes in the Book of Daniel," *Journal of the Adventist Theological Society* 7, no. 1 (1996): 21–39.

7. William G. Johnsson, "Biblical Apocalyptic," in *Handbook of Seventh-day Adventist Theology*, ed. Raoul Dederen (Hagerstown, MD: Review and Herald®, 2000), 784–814.

8. Johnsson, "Biblical Apocalyptic," 784–814.

9. *Seventh-day Adventist Encyclopedia*, 2nd rev. ed. (Hagerstown, MD: Review and Herald®, 1995), s.v. "Historicism."

10. *Seventh-day Adventist Encyclopedia*, s.v. "Historicism."

11. *Seventh-day Adventist Encyclopedia*, s.v. "Historicism."

12. William H. Shea, *Selected Studies on Prophetic Interpretation*, vol. 1, rev. ed., Daniel and Revelation Committee Series (Silver Spring, MD: Biblical Research Institute, 1992), 72.

13. Alberto R. Timm, "Miniature Symbolization and the Year-Day Principle of Prophetic Interpretation," *Andrews University Seminary Studies* 42, no. 1 (2004): 166.

14. Timm, "Miniature Symbolization," 166.

15. Ellen G. White, "Knowing God," *Youth's Instructor*, April 7, 1908, 13.

16. Abraham Kuyper, *Abraham Kuyper: A Centennial Reader*, ed. James D. Bratt (Grand Rapids, MI: Eerdmans, 1998), 488; emphasis in the original.

17. George R. Knight, *The Apocalyptic Vision and the Neutering of Adventism* (Hagerstown, MD: Review and Herald®, 2008), 37, 38.

CHAPTER 2

From Jerusalem to Babylon

The book of Daniel opens on the gloomy note of Nebuchadnezzar's invasion of Judah. In this initial conquest, the king of Babylon defeated Jerusalem, took captives, and confiscated the sacred vessels of the temple. At first glance, these events give the impression that the God of Judah had been defeated by the gods of Babylon. However, a closer reading shows that the defeat of Jerusalem was an act of God. "And the Lord gave Jehoiakim king of Judah into his [Nebuchadnezzar's] hand" (Daniel 1:2). This comment sets the theological tone for Daniel's entire message. It is the God of Judah who sovereignly rules over the kingdoms of the world, establishing and removing kings according to His will. Because God's people had broken the covenant and rejected repeated invitations to restore their relationship with God, the Lord sent Babylonian armies to dismantle their society. Over the course of seventy years, Judah suffered three consecutive invasions; the Promised Land lay desolate, and its inhabitants were exiled to Babylon.

During the first invasion in 605 B.C., Daniel and his friends were carried off to Babylon. Given the refusal of the Judahite king to submit to the Babylonians, Nebuchadnezzar ordered another attack in 597 B.C. On that occasion, the Babylonian king replaced King Jehoiakim with Zedekiah and brought to

Babylon "all the treasures of the house of the LORD and the treasures of the king's house, and he cut in pieces all the articles of gold which Solomon king of Israel had made in the temple of the LORD" (2 Kings 24:13). Nebuchadnezzar also took another group of captives, including King Jehoiakim and the prophet Ezekiel. Unfortunately, Zedekiah spurned the lesson to submit fully to Babylon. As a result, Nebuchadnezzar returned to Jerusalem and razed it, burning the temple and marching another group of exiles to Babylon.

It must have been painful for the people to experience the collapse of the three covenantal institutions that gave meaning to their lives. First, Solomon's majestic temple, the locus of God's presence among them, was sacked and eventually destroyed by the enemy. Second, the Davidic king came under the yoke of Nebuchadnezzar and was eventually taken captive to Babylon. And last, their homeland—given to them under the terms of the Abrahamic covenant—came under the control of a foreign power. Many of its inhabitants, including Daniel and his friends, were banished to a foreign land, people, language, and culture.

Against this dismal backdrop of desolation, destruction, and apparent divine abandonment, Daniel and his companions demonstrated unswerving loyalty to the God of their fathers. Though it seemed God had abandoned His people, these four young men remained courageously firm. They looked beyond their circumstances to the transcendent God who was able to reverse the disaster and bring healing to His people.

God's faithfulness to Daniel

As the book of Daniel unfolds, it becomes clear that what Babylon took away, God restored a thousand times over. In contrast to the subjugation of Judah by Babylon, the God of heaven is portrayed as a stone filling the whole earth like a mountain—a fitting image of an eternal kingdom that will replace all earthly kingdoms and human powers (Daniel 2). Though Babylon brought Jehoiakim, the son of David, under its vassalage and eventually into captivity, the Son of man will receive an eternal kingdom and share His royal power with the saints of the Most High in the end (Daniel 7). Likewise, whereas Babylon desecrated and eventually destroyed the glorious temple built by Solomon, God will purify the heavenly temple and bestow justice and salvation on His people (Daniel 8). And while the forces of Babylon may succeed in storming earthly Zion, God will ultimately obliterate the forces of evil as they attempt to overtake the "glorious holy mountain" (Daniel 11:45). While enemy armies may defeat and displace God's people, He assures us that in the time of the end Michael will rise and defend His people against the forces that oppose and persecute them (Daniel 12). Thus, the dismal picture of defeat and destruction found in the beginning gives way to scenes of restoration, purification, and salvation. In a glorious climax, death itself is defeated as God brings to life those who sleep in the dust (Daniel 12).

God's promise to reverse the Exile of His people over the long sweep of history is evidenced in His care for Daniel and his companions. As they faced the challenges of living in Nebuchadnezzar's Babylon, God was with them. He heard their prayers and influenced the Babylonian authorities to grant the request of God's captive servants, proving that He was not geographically limited to the temple or the Promised Land. He abides with His people wherever they are because He is the Lord and Creator of the entire earth.

Moreover, God caused His children to thrive in this strange land. As the Bible says, God influenced the chief of the eunuchs to grant Daniel's request for a vegetarian diet in lieu of food from the king's table. A ten-day test was granted, and God blessed the captives with better health than all the other candidates in the king's service. The biblical narrative uses the expression "fatter in flesh" to describe their healthy glow, which is to say that they looked better than all the other young men who ate from the king's table (Daniel 1:15). Interestingly, this is the same phrase employed to describe the appearance of the first seven cows in Pharaoh's dream, symbolizing seven years of prosperity for Egypt under Joseph's management (Genesis 41:18). Incidentally, this linguistic link with the Joseph narrative may hint at God bestowing prosperity on Babylon through the leadership of Daniel and his friends in the kingdom's administration.

As revealed in the covenant, the children of Abraham were to be a blessing to all the families of the earth. Ultimately, this promise finds its fulfillment in Christ as the Gentiles are incorporated into God's people. When modern Christians perform acts of kindness to non-Christian neighbors, they are acting like Daniel and Joseph, fulfilling God's plan to bless all the families of the earth.

God not only gave wisdom and outstanding intellectual skills to Daniel and his friends but blessed Daniel with the supernatural gift of interpreting visions and dreams. At the end of the training period, it is no wonder that the Babylonian king found Daniel and his friends "ten times better than all the magicians and astrologers who were in all his realm" (Daniel 1:20).

Of course, the main protagonist of the book is not Daniel, Nebuchadnezzar, Darius, or Cyrus but God Himself. It is the Sovereign of the universe who emerges as the hero of the book. Under the terms of the covenant, God brought judgment upon His people but never abandoned them. He allowed Nebuchadnezzar to bring His people to Babylon, but He also came to Babylon to dwell with them. For the inhabitants of Babylon, and perhaps even for the exiles, the God of Israel may have seemed indifferent or oblivious to the plight of His people. In spite of external appearances, God was acting behind the scenes, guiding and directing world events and the personal lives of His servants. His unfailing faithfulness to Daniel was a reward to Daniel's faith in Him.

In the same way, we can face life's troubles and challenges with the assurance that God is always faithful to His promises. Even if He seems indifferent to our personal problems, we can rest assured that the God of Daniel remains our God. He not only drives history to its climax but takes personal interest in each of His children.

Daniel's faithfulness to God

As a young man, Daniel faced daunting challenges yet remained loyal to the God of his fathers. Upon arriving in Babylon, Daniel and his companions were selected for special training for service in the Babylonian court. Not surprisingly, it was the practice of ancient emperors to select the best youth of subjugated peoples to serve in the royal court. This strategy allowed the emperors to maintain dominion over their vassals without straining their army.

The process of training foreigners to serve in the royal palace involved much more than practical expertise and technical knowledge. In fact, candidates for royal service underwent indoctrination designed to change their worldview and win them over to the ideology of the empire. In the case of Daniel and his friends, this ideological conversion involved two main aspects. First, their names were changed. In Hebrew, the names of Daniel, Hananiah, Mishael, and Azariah contained references to the God of Israel (El, Yahweh). In a direct attempt to change their thinking, the Babylonians called them Belteshazzar, Shadrach, Meshach, and Abed-Nego; these names expressed a praising reference to such gods of Babylon as Bel, Nabu, and Aku. Every time someone would call their names, they would be reminded of the corresponding Babylonian deity.

Apparently, the Hebrew worthies did not oppose the new names. They probably perceived such names as mere labels, with little bearing on their faith and commitment to the true God. Their loyalty to Him stemmed from their hearts rather than a name or a label assigned to them.

But the other aspect of the conversion process was rejected. They could not participate in eating food from the king's table. The biblical text does not explain the reasons for their refusal. Among several opinions offered by commentators, the most likely explanation is that the food may have been offered to the Babylonian gods. Besides, accepting food from the king's table meant dependence on the king and acquiescence to his ideology. Such a step the Hebrew captives could not make without compromising their loyalty to the Lord. Therefore, they requested that the menu provided by the king be replaced with a simple vegetarian diet, which resembled the diet established by God at Creation. This arrangement highlighted their dependence on God for their physical health and enhanced their success in the educational process.

As we reflect on the courageous resistance of Daniel and his companions, a significant lesson emerges. Early childhood training is crucial. The Hebrew captives flourished because they were solidly grounded in the Hebraic worldview. They were quite young when enrolled in the royal training and service (Daniel may have only been sixteen to eighteen years old), far from their land and culture. They were vulnerable. There was immense pressure for them to render allegiance to Babylonian ideology, but, being well-trained in the faith of their parents, they never swayed. Their worldview, their understanding of God's character, and their grasp of God's actions in Israel's history kept them on solid ground. The God who acted on behalf of Daniel and his companions is the same God who can and will do similar things for families today.

The example of the Hebrew captives establishes a paradigm for living in the contemporary culture, and at least three areas deserve mention. First, as Seventh-day Adventist Christians, we hold the Bible as God's Word and cherish fundamental beliefs that distinguish us from other religious movements and denominations. However, assent to a set of such beliefs is not enough. They must be integrated into a distinctive worldview. More specifically, our views on God, the great controversy, sin, salvation, God's law, the sanctuary, and last things (eschatology) form an integrated system of beliefs that provide a biblical perspective on reality, helping us to resist the sinful allurements of the world.

Second, like Daniel, we must be aware of lifestyle matters. What we eat, what we wear, what we see, and where we go are an expression of our ultimate loyalty. Informed by Scripture and guided by the Holy Spirit, we should live in ways consistent with God's will.

And third, retreating from society and culture is not a viable option. Like Daniel, we must account for our faith in the fray of real life. We must live our lives in constant interaction with culture and society. The challenge of living as God's children in a hostile culture is immense. It requires wisdom to choose the right way and to do the right thing. How can you mingle with non-Christian neighbors without being affected by their lifestyles? Where are the limits, and what lines should be drawn? In what ways does your cultural context determine your decisions on these matters?

As you face these issues, you can rely on God-given wisdom and discernment to live a Christian life in your culture. Whatever the circumstances may be, we are called to interact with sinners, showing them what God has accomplished in our lives and attracting them to new lives in Christ.

Conclusion

A young Christian woman once worked as a quality-control inspector at a pharmaceutical company. One day, due to faulty procedures, a major order of syringes was contaminated and failed inspection. When she reported the contamination to her boss, he quickly calculated the expense of reproducing the order and made a cost-effective decision: ship the order. He ordered her to sign the clearance forms, despite the contamination. She refused. To complicate things further, because of government regulations, she was the only one that could sign the clearance. The syringes did not ship that day, and a few days later, because of her refusal to compromise, she was fired. Like Daniel and his friends, she made a costly decision.

In one way or another, each of us faces pressure—pressure from our spouse, relatives, friends, bosses, or competitors. There may even be pressure from within, pressure from our own desire for success and significance.

What about the young woman who lost her job? God never abandoned her. Because she refused to sign the clearance forms for the contaminated syringes, the order was not delivered to the customer on time. Some company officials investigated the delay and discovered that she had protected them from the contaminated syringes, even at the cost of her own job. The company for which the syringes were intended was so appreciative that they hired her with increased pay.[1]

Although we can rest assured that the Lord never abandons those who are faithful to Him, the reward for loyalty is not always immediate. Faithfulness may cost a job, academic growth, a friendship, or a family relationship. The long gallery of Christian martyrs shows that deliverance in this life is not always the case, but whatever the circumstances, the Lord will never forget His loyal children.

---

1. Adapted from Bryan Chapell, *The Gospel According to Daniel: A Christ-Centered Approach* (Grand Rapids, MI: Baker Books, 2014), 14–23.

CHAPTER 3

From Mystery to Revelation

After graduating summa cum laude from the "University of Babylon," Daniel faced an impossible task. He was called upon to interpret a dream that was troubling King Nebuchadnezzar. There was only one catch: the king would not report the dream. Daniel 2 tells the story of Babylon's wise men jockeying for position, scrambling to meet the king's demands. Their high-stakes failure to tell the dream and its interpretation jeopardized their own lives and the lives of all the counselors, including Daniel and his friends. Learning of their shared fate, Daniel went to his knees, pleading for wisdom to understand the dream and its interpretation. God graciously revealed everything to Daniel, and the day was saved; Nebuchadnezzar's wrath was averted.

This dramatic story sets the stage for the king's dream. What soon becomes clear is that God is the ultimate protagonist of human history. He has a plan for the world, and He communicates truth in ways that humans can understand. He reveals the broad sweep of human history, from the Babylonian Empire up to the end of the world, assuring us that He stands in charge of human affairs.

How God communicates

One of the fascinating aspects of God's interaction with human beings lies in the fact that He can and often does communicate with humankind. From Daniel 2, we learn that God gave King Nebuchadnezzar a dream and revealed its interpretation to Daniel. The fact that God speaks to us and provides us with concrete and objective information constitutes one of the most challenging concepts for modern and postmodern people. It seems easier to accept the idea that God relates to us in mystical, nonverbal, or experiential ways than to accept the biblical teaching that He speaks and communicates objective information. However, the book of Daniel embraces the idea that God reveals objective information about the future and our experience with Him—a God who steers the course of history and discloses events before they happen.

A close examination of the biblical narrative reveals another facet of God's relationship with us: He speaks in ways and in language that humans can understand. In communicating with the Babylonian king in a dream, God used a familiar and impressive method to reach the monarch. Ancient Near Eastern rulers were obsessed with dreams. For this reason, the ancient Babylonians had a special class of scholars who specialized in the interpretation of dreams. In the ancient world, a dream was never considered the result of a hearty dinner but was a communication from the gods.[1] Understanding this, God gave a dream to Nebuchadnezzar because He knew the king would take it seriously. "Dreams in the ancient world were thought to offer information from the divine realm and were therefore taken very seriously. Some dreams given to prophets and kings were considered a means of divine revelation. Most dreams, however, the ordinary dreams of common people, were believed to contain omens that communicated information about what the gods were doing."[2]

Second, God used the imagery of a statue—a revered and prominent element in Nebuchadnezzar's culture. The Greek historian Herodotus mentions a solid-gold statue in the temple of Bel in Babylon. As noted in scholarly literature, dreams involving statues are attested of in Egypt and Mesopotamia and usually evoke kings going to war.[3] This is an interesting point, considering that the dream given to Nebuchadnezzar occurred during the period of the consolidation of his empire. In addition, ancient Babylonian statues sometimes combined different metals, such as bronze and iron, that were covered with gold and silver. Interestingly, four-metal symbolism existed in the ancient world before Daniel's time. The Greek poet Hesiod (ca. 700 B.C.) wrote of ages of gold, silver, bronze, and iron.[4] However, as has been noted,

> Significant differences do exist between the book of Daniel and Hesiod's work: 1. Hesiod inserted an Age of Heroes between the Bronze and the Iron ages. Thus, he arrived "at five ages between the time of man's innocence and his own day: gold, silver, bronze, the age of heroes, iron." 2. In Hesiod's work we have a sequence of five transient empires; in Daniel 2 a fifth empire of eternal duration follows the four world ones. 3. Hesiod's predictions do not lead to an eschatological climax, while in Daniel 2 everything builds up to it.[5]

What God showed Nebuchadnezzar in the dream was a combination of elements already known to the king, mixed with a few completely new aspects. One unique facet of Nebuchadnezzar's dream is that it represents the flow of history and not a god or a king. Another feature, even more distinctive, is the stone cut from the mountain (verse 45). All the previous transitions had been rather ordinary in nature, with one metal replacing another. But in the closing scene, the stone strikes the image's feet and destroys it. After a wind carries away the rubble, the mysterious stone grows into a great mountain, filling the earth. It absorbs all previous earthly kingdoms and never suffers destruction.

All of this demonstrates that God not only communicates truth to human beings but does so on a level they can understand. Blending familiar and unfamiliar images, God was able to communicate with the pagan king and effectively reach modern people.

What God communicates

Daniel 2, the first prophetic outline in the book of Daniel, climaxes with the establishment of God's kingdom. All the subsequent outlines fit into the prophetic scheme of this chapter, introducing and developing distinctive emphases. Chapter 7 repeats the sequence of the four kingdoms of chapter 2 but culminates with the Son of man as the Ancient of Days performs judgment in heaven. Chapter 8 picks up human history in the Persian era and reaches a climactic point with the purification of the heavenly sanctuary. The last prophetic outline traces a more detailed account of human history—from Persian times to when Michael rises to deliver God's people (Daniel 12:1–4), obliterating evil and God's enemies in the "glorious holy mountain" (Daniel 11:45).

The prophetic outline, conveyed through the image shown to Nebuchadnezzar, follows the history of the world from the time of the Babylonian Empire until the establishment of God's eternal kingdom. As the first of four prophetic outlines—the others being chapters 7; 8, 9; and 10–12—Daniel 2 sets the basic pattern for the subsequent prophetic outlines revealed to Daniel. Although coming from a different perspective, the prophecies conveyed by Daniel 7–12 are expansions and developments of the prophecy of Daniel 2.[6]

The dream displayed a "great image, whose splendor was excellent" (Daniel 2:31). It consisted of a multilayered work of metals: head of gold, chest and arms of silver, belly and thighs of bronze, legs of iron, and feet partly of iron and partly of clay. From head and shoulders to knees and toes, the metals decrease in value yet increase in strength, save for the toes of iron and clay.

From Daniel's interpretation and the historical record, the following outline emerges:

Head of gold. Nebuchadnezzar personified the Neo-Babylonian Empire (605–539 B.C.). The expansion of the Babylonian Empire and the splendor of Babylon owed much to his military and administrative skills. In addition, an abundance of gold embellished the palaces and temples of Babylon.

Chest and arms of silver. As silver is inferior to gold, so the Medo-Persian Empire (539–331 B.C.) is inferior in luxury and magnificence. Interestingly, the Persians used silver in their taxation system. Although some interpreters refer to the second kingdom as the Median Empire alone (with Persia as the third), we should note that there was no separate Median Empire between the Babylonian and Persian Empires.

Belly and thighs of bronze. The third empire refers to the Greek Empire (331–168 B.C.) established by Alexander the Great. Greek soldiers were noted for their brazen armor. In addition, their helmets, shields, and battle-axes were made of brass.

Legs of iron. This metal is a fitting representation for Rome (168 B.C.–A.D. 476), a power stronger than all of its predecessors. Its iron fist crushed all who dared resist its advance. Rome ruled more territory and lasted longer than all the empires before it.

Feet partly of iron and partly of clay. This symbol indicates that the iron empire of Rome would be degraded. From the ruins of the Western Roman Empire, conquered by barbarian invasions (later followed by the fall of the Eastern Roman Empire to the Ottoman Turks), arose the modern nations of Europe. Today, those nations remain divided despite centuries of attempts to unite them by means of political alliances and intermarriages. Although some suggest that the toes should correspond to the ten horns of the fourth beast of chapter 7, it is more plausible to understand them as a general symbol without mathematical precision. The mix of iron with clay points to a situation of fragmentation and a precarious unity that would prevail in the period between the collapse of the fourth kingdom and the establishment of the stone kingdom. Ellen White also applies the iron-clay feet to the mingling of church and state manifested in the papacy.[7] This application seems consistent with the historical developments of the papacy, its rise to power, and the profound influence it exerted on the politics of Europe after the demise of the Roman Empire.

Stone. The climactic point of the king's prophetic dream was a mysterious rock, carved from a mountain. Scripture applies the metaphor of the stone to Jesus Christ (1 Corinthians 10:4; Isaiah 28:16; Luke 20:17, 18). As the book of Daniel explains, the symbolism of the stone represents the establishment of God's eternal kingdom. Some commentators apply this prophetic event to the first coming of Jesus and the spread of the gospel to the world. However, the stone's demolition of the image, beginning at its feet and toes, points to an event occurring after the demise of the Roman Empire. For this reason, the stone must represent the second coming of Jesus, when the kingdoms of the earth will be replaced with God's eternal kingdom.

Why God communicates

In the study of Bible prophecy, it is possible to become so absorbed with dates and details that attention is diverted from the One driving the flow of history and prophetic events. Historical information in prophecy is important because it identifies God's guiding hand at work in the human story. However, prophetic chronology's primary function is to draw hearts to the ultimate protagonist of prophetic events—the God of the universe.

In this regard, the prophetic outline of Daniel 2 reveals a number of insights into God's activity on behalf of His people. Broadly speaking, He manifests Himself as the Lord of history, who transcends political maneuvering, power struggles, and the parade of world empires, eventually establishing His kingdom.

As we ponder the political and economic challenges of the world today, we must remember that nations and rulers are in God's hands. It is He who ultimately directs the course of human history. Current events can be discouraging, but God is still in charge. He not only speaks but also hears the prayers of His children.

As Daniel 2's narrative makes clear, Nebuchadnezzar was about to execute all the sages of Babylon, including Daniel and his friends. Upon hearing the decree, Daniel went to his knees, pleading for a miracle. In response to God's dramatic deliverance, he penned this poem:

"Blessed be the name of God forever and ever,
For wisdom and might are His.
And He changes the times and the seasons;
He removes kings and raises up kings;
He gives wisdom to the wise
And knowledge to those who have understanding.
He reveals deep and secret things;
He knows what is in the darkness,
And light dwells with Him.

"I thank You and praise You,
O God of my fathers;
You have given me wisdom and might,
And have now made known to me what we asked of You,
For You have made known to us the king's demand" (Daniel 2:20–23).

Note that Daniel makes significant assertions about God. God is worthy of praise because of His wisdom and might. God changes the times, seasons, and kings. God reveals deep and secret things. God gives wisdom. Such affirmations are in stark contrast to the Babylonian gods, who were powerless to perform any of these functions (Isaiah 44:9–22). These bold declarations are reassuring and should encourage us to praise God for who He is and for what He does. He deserves our praise in good times and bad. Regardless of our circumstances, He always deserves our worship.

God's work in Daniel's life follows a familiar pattern. Daniel's stand before Nebuchadnezzar shares similarities with the story of Joseph before Pharaoh. Both Joseph and Daniel lived at crucial times in the history of God's people. Joseph served in Egypt before Israel possessed the Promised Land, and Daniel served in Babylon after they lost it. In both situations, God gave dreams to foreign kings that could be interpreted only by His faithful servants. As one scholar summarizes: "Both monarchs had disturbing dreams from God that revealed the future

(Gen. 41:25; Dan. 2:28–29, 45). Both young exiles demonstrated the superiority of their God and succeeded where royal experts failed. Both captives denied superior ability and credited God with their knowledge (Gen. 41:16; Dan. 2:30). Onlookers believed the men's ability resulted from the 'spirit of the holy gods' in them (Gen. 41:38; cf. Dan. 2:11; 4:8, 18). Both Daniel and Joseph achieved great political power because of their royal service (Gen. 41:39–46; Daniel 2:48)."[8]

Finally, it bears noting that, having received the dream's interpretation from Daniel, King Nebuchadnezzar "fell on his face, prostrate before Daniel, and commanded that they should present an offering and incense to him" (Daniel 2:46). Such a gesture does not mean that Nebuchadnezzar treated Daniel as a deity or gave him the adoration worthy of a god. Indeed, in the context of Babylonian culture, this procedure expressed the natural reaction of the king, who was recognizing Daniel's valor as a trustworthy spokesman for the God of heaven. Therefore, Nebuchadnezzar exalted Daniel to a quasi-royal position and bestowed honors worthy of a king upon the prophet.[9]

Conclusion

Israelites living during the Exile were not abandoned by God, but they may have felt that way. Likewise, given our present political, economic, or social circumstances, we may be tempted to think that God has left the world to itself. Daniel 2 speaks clearly to our predicament. No matter what happens, God remains sovereign. History is not a mere succession of world empires, rising and falling at the pace of human whim. Indeed, every nation, potentate, and government stands under God's ultimate sovereignty. Soon, all world powers will be replaced by God's eternal kingdom. He who uttered the first word of Creation will have the last word in history. We can live with hope, knowing that God holds the future.

---

1. See Leo Oppenheim, "The Interpretation of Dreams in the Ancient Near East, With a Translation of an Assyrian Dream-Book," *Transactions of the American*

Philosophical Society 46, no. 3 (1956): 179–373.

2. John H. Walton, Victor H. Matthews, and Mark W. Chavalas, *The IVP Bible Background Commentary: Old Testament* (Downers Grove, IL: InterVarsity Press, 2000), 572.

3. John J. Collins, *Daniel: A Commentary on the Book of Daniel*, Hermeneia (Minneapolis, MN: Fortress, 1994), 165.

4. Hugh G. Evelyn-White, trans., *Hesiod*, in *Hesiod, the Homeric Hymns and Homerica,* (Cambridge, MA: Harvard University Press, 1959), lines 140–200.

5. Gerhard Pfandl, *Daniel: The Seer of Babylon* (Hagerstown, MD: Review and Herald®, 2004), 22.

6. Brevard S. Childs, *Introduction to the Old Testament as Scripture* (Philadelphia: Fortress, 1979), 618.

7. Ellen G. White, Manuscript 63, 1899, quoted in *Manuscript Releases*, vol. 15 (Silver Spring, MD: Ellen G. White Estate, 1990), 39.

8. Wendy L. Widder, *Daniel*, Story of God Bible Commentary (Grand Rapids, MI: Zondervan, 2016), 55.

9. Alan Millard, "Incense—the Ancient Room Freshener: The Exegesis of Daniel 2:46," in *On Stone and Scroll: Essays in Honour of Graham Ivor Davies*, ed. James K. Aitken, Katharine J. Dell, and Brian A. Mastin (Berlin: De Gruyter, 2011), 111–122.

CHAPTER 4

From Furnace to Palace

The story of the three Hebrew captives thrown into the fiery furnace has stirred the imaginations of commentators, artists, and preachers. Often, the retelling of the story focuses on the deliverance of the three young men from the flames. While the narrative does highlight their deliverance, the main focus of the passage is on God's unswerving faithfulness to Israel. Indeed, verses 16–18 of Daniel 3 lie at the center of the literary structure of the narrative. They describe the faithful Jews confronting the king and telling him they would rather die than worship the image.

A. Nebuchadnezzar's decree to worship the golden image (verses 1–7)
  B. The Jews accused (verses 8–12)
    C. The Jews threatened (verses 13–15)
      D. The Jews confess their faith (verses 16–18)
    C.' The Jews punished (verses 19–23)
  B.' The Jews vindicated (verses 24–27)
A.' Nebuchadnezzar's decree honoring the Jews and their God (verses 28–30)[1]

Gaps in the story

A few gaps in the story raise questions that have no simple answers. One such question relates to the meaning and message of the towering image. References to the "image" set up by Nebuchadnezzar appear ten times in the text (verses 1, 2, 3, 5, 7, 10, 12, 14, 15, 18), and yet the narrative seems vague about its features and purpose. The suggestion has been made that the image may have been intended to mark a special event in the reign of the king. As one scholar states: "Ancient Near Eastern kings built many monuments, statues, and temples—often to symbolize their power or praise their gods—and celebratory ceremonies often accompanied such projects."[2]

Moreover, it is not clear whether it was an image of a god or of the king himself. But because Mesopotamian kings were not regarded as deities (as was the case in Egypt), most scholars think that the statue may have represented a deity. This being so, one may theorize that the majestic image represented a god such as Marduk or Nabu. By erecting that image and requiring all of his officers to pay homage to it, the king may have intended to compel his subjects' loyalty to the religion and ideology of the empire. It bears noting that in ancient times religion and politics were inextricably intertwined.

Another point relates to the nature of such an unusual and disproportional statue. Measuring 60 cubits tall by 6 cubits wide (90 feet tall by 9 feet wide), such a figure probably looked more like an obelisk or a pillar than a human-shaped image. But whatever the case, large statues were not unusual in ancient times. Some statues built by early Egyptian pharaohs could reach up to 60 feet in height. A statue of Zeus, located in Olympia, Greece, stood almost 40 feet high, while the Colossus on the island of Rhodes was 105 feet tall. So it is plausible that Nebuchadnezzar erected a large statue.[3]

Another question to be addressed concerns the identity of the fourth man that appears in the midst of the fire, along with the three faithful young men. Nebuchadnezzar refers to this person as a "Son of God" (verse 25), or a divine being. Given Nebuchadnezzar's polytheistic outlook, he certainly did not mean the

Hebrew God when he used the Aramaic plural for "gods" (*'ĕlāhîm*). He also refers to the fourth figure as an "angel" (verse 28), which may have prompted the rabbinic tradition to associate the fourth man with Gabriel.[4] Several church fathers however, identified the fourth man with the preincarnate Christ,[5] a view also held by Ellen G. White[6] and several conservative commentators.[7] That being the case, the fourth man is to be identified with the same heavenly being who later appears in the book of Daniel as Son of man (Daniel 7), the Prince of the host (Daniel 8), Messiah (Daniel 9), and Michael (Daniel 12).

A final point concerns the whereabouts of Daniel during the episode in Daniel 3. Considering the prestige of Daniel, it seems difficult to account for his absence at the convocation on the Plain of Dura. Although several hypotheses have been advanced, such as business travel, illness, or even God's intention to keep him away from the event, the fact is we do not know. However, this should not distract us from the message of the narrative. What we can assert with certainty is that Daniel either did not worship the image or was not present at the ceremony.

Imposing false worship

A striking aspect of this story is the absolute irrevocability of the decree to worship the image. The mention of the names of the various officials occurs twice in the space of two verses, as if to make it absolutely clear that no exceptions were allowed: satraps, administrators, governors, counselors, treasurers, judges, magistrates, and all the officials of the provinces (verses 2, 3). Additionally, such repetition also shows that the officials were requested to act automatically, in obedience to Nebuchadnezzar's command to worship the image.

In terms of the audience, the demands to worship the image were comprehensive. Instructions for the adoration of the statue follow the same pattern. A herald cries out that when the people hear "the sound of the horn, flute, harp, lyre, and psaltery, in symphony with all kinds of music," they should fall down and worship the image (verse 5). This list of musical instruments appears four times in the story and is always followed by the threat to punish those who refuse to obey. The instruments appear in the opening instructions, when the actual worship takes place, in the accusation against the three young men, and finally when the king offers the three captives a second chance.

Such repetitions convey the idea of a mechanical process as the worshipers are guided by the external commands of the liturgy. The worship is not voluntary, springing from a convicted conscience. The picture emerges of a huge crowd robotically touching their noses to the ground at the mechanical sound of the orchestra. One author argues that the entire narrative intends to make the grand occasion promoted by Nebuchadnezzar look silly, as the pagans respond to the adoration commands like Pavlov's dog.[8]

The worship system established by Nebuchadnezzar was enforced under the penalty of death. Whoever refused to abide by the determinations of the king would be thrown into a blazing furnace. It is possible that such a furnace was the one used to shape the image, and for convenience, it was turned into an instrument of execution. Whatever the case, the king uses "the furnace as a weapon of opportunity."[9] Indeed, "no clear details are given about the furnace. Verses 22–23 may indicate that it had an opening at the top through which the victims were thrown into the fire, and there seems to have been a door or opening in the side through which Nebuchadnezzar could see into it (3:24)."[10]

The narrative shows how far a despot can go to impose his will on fellow human beings. By setting up a system of false worship, the king dehumanized his subjects, causing the worshipers to think and act like automated entities. In doing so, the egomaniacal monarch became an idol himself. Idolatry, the worship of an image deity, ultimately undermines the only legitimate image of God—the human being (Genesis 1:26–28).

Today, we may not face the danger of a despotic ruler imposing the adoration of an external image. But we may face the no less serious temptations of replacing the true God with the idols of the contemporary world. Idolatry is not only around us but often springs from within. We must constantly resist the idols of consumerism, technology, individualism, and hedonism. Our contemporary culture often imposes the adoration of these idols with no less power than that of Nebuchadnezzar.

Resisting false worship

As the story continues, the large crowd bows to the image of gold, save for the three who refused to compromise. According to Daniel 3's literary structure, the fulcrum of the story lies in verses 16–18. These verses depict the extraordinary courage of Daniel's three friends, who refused to conform to the king's will. Again, the narrative is not primarily about their liberation from the fire but rather about their determination to confront the king and remain faithful to God. A few points are worth mentioning in this regard.

First, the men are consistently referred to as Shadrach, Meshach, and Abed-Nego. The use of their Babylonian names, a clear attempt to deny their Hebrew identity, makes them even more vulnerable. However, they act and react according to the identity conveyed by their Hebrew names: Hananiah (God is gracious), Mishael (who is like God?), and Azariah (the Lord helps).

Second, it must be noted that the three Hebrews were under intense peer pressure. They were on display before the king, the royal officers, and a crowd of spectators.

Third, attention must be turned to the climactic scene: "Shadrach, Meshach, and Abed-Nego answered and said to the king, 'O Nebuchadnezzar, we have no need to answer you in this matter. If that is the case, our God whom we serve is able to deliver us from the burning fiery furnace, and He will deliver us from your hand, O king. But if not, let it be known to you, O king, that we do not serve your gods, nor will we worship the gold image which you have set up' " (Daniel 3:16–18).

The conditional sentence that begins in verse 17 has drawn intense interest because in Aramaic it literally reads: "If our God whom we serve exists, He is able to deliver us from the burning fiery furnace, and He will deliver us from your hand, O king." But this conditional clause ("If our God . . .") should not be understood as casting doubt on God's existence. Rather, the three young man are simply stating, as one commentator explains, a conditional thought: "If their God exists—the God of Israel, who had revealed his Law and spoken his gracious Gospel words of promise through Moses and the Prophets—then it follows that he has the power to save them. The conditional sentence does not (contrary to the perception of many) call into question the premise of God's existence. It simply draws the conclusion—that God can save them—based on the premise that their saving God exists."[11]

The next verse shows the extent of their conviction: "But if not, let it be known to you, O king, that we do not serve your gods, nor will we worship the gold image which you have set up" (verse 18). That is, if for some reason God was not willing to save them, they preferred death over surrendering to the idolatrous demands of the king. In obedience to the first two commandments and the Shema (Deuteronomy 6:4), they had purposed in their hearts to reject idolatry and worship God alone. They are not certain that God will deliver them from death, nor do they demand it. Instead, they entrust themselves to Him and choose not to worship the image. This obedience, motivated by principle rather than convenience, was the expression of a fireproof faith.

Vindicating loyalty

As the sentence was executed, and the three young men were cast into the blazing furnace, the king puzzled over the presence of a fourth man in the fire. Nebuchadnezzar immediately recognized the figure as a supernatural being sent from the divine realm. As mentioned above, there is good reason to identify the fourth man with the preincarnate Christ. God, in His infinite wisdom and love, vindicated the three young men by sparing their lives. And as the Son of God entered the furnace—whose temperature may have "ranged from 1,650 to 2,700 degrees Fahrenheit"[12]—the fire lost its power.

At first glance, one could gather that deliverance from the fire stands as the main point of the story. However, as already alluded to, the vindication of the three Hebrews does not primarily lie in their deliverance but in the presence of God's Son with them. This point is crucial because on other occasions, God's servants have sealed their testimony with death. Were they abandoned? Were they less favored than the three Hebrew worthies? Not at all, because Jesus has promised to always be with us, "even unto the end of the world" (Matthew 28:20, ASV). We are never left alone. And yet, while the sojourn continues, the faithful will face fiery trials and take part in Christ's sufferings (1 Peter 4:12–14).

But even when vindication does not come with immediate deliverance from physical pain and death, God grants to all His children ultimate validation in the heavenly temple. While we face trials and persecution in this world, we can look to Jesus and be encouraged by His promise: "Do not fear any of those things which you are about to suffer. Indeed, the devil is about to throw some of you into prison, that you may be tested, and you will have tribulation ten days. Be faithful until death, and I will give you the crown of life" (Revelation 2:10).

Conclusion

From the reign of the Roman emperor Licinius I (A.D. 308–324) comes the story of forty Christian soldiers who gave a powerful testimony of unwavering allegiance to Christ. They were members of the Twelfth Legion, which was stationed at Sebaste in Armenia.[13] One day their captain told them Emperor Licinius had sent out an edict that all soldiers were to offer sacrifice to the pagan gods. These Christians replied, "You can have our armor and even our bodies, but our hearts' allegiance belongs to Jesus Christ." It was midwinter of A.D. 320, and the captain had them marched onto a nearby frozen lake. He stripped them of their clothes and decreed they would either die or renounce Christ.

Throughout the night, these men huddled together, singing their song, "Forty martyrs for Christ." One by one the temperature took its toll and they fell to the ice. At last there was only one man left. He lost courage and stumbled to the shore, where he renounced Christ. The officer of the guards had been watching all this. Unknown to the others, he had secretly come to believe in Christ. When he saw this last man break rank, he walked out onto the ice, threw off his clothes, and confessed that he also was a Christian. When the sun rose the next morning, there were forty bodies of soldiers who had fought to the death for Christ.[14]

The three Hebrew captives were not thrown onto a frozen lake but into a fiery furnace. Although they were eventually rescued, they were no less willing to lay down their lives for God than the forty martyrs of Sebaste. Under immense peer pressure, they remained faithful to the end.

This story's call to action is much greater than to "dare to be like Shadrach, Meshach, and Abed-Nego." It is rather a summons to "dare to believe that God is worthy of your fidelity in any challenge that confronts you, for his name's sake." Whether in life or in death, let us remain faithful to our Lord and Savior.

---

1. Ernest C. Lucas, *Daniel*, Apollos Old Testament Commentary, vol. 20 (Downers Grove, IL: InterVarsity Press, 2002), 86.
2. Wendy L. Widder, *Daniel*, Story of God Bible Commentary (Grand Rapids, MI: Zondervan, 2016), 68.
3. Stephen R. Miller, *Daniel*, The New American Commentary, vol. 18 (Nashville: Broadman & Holman, 1994), 109.
4. Jacob Neusner, ed., *The Babylonian Talmud: A Translation and Commentary* (Peabody, MA: Hendrickson, 2011), 4:547 (b. Pesah. 118A, B).
5. See Kenneth Stevenson and Michael Glerup, eds., *Ezekiel, Daniel*, Ancient Christian Commentary on Scripture, vol. 13 (Downers Grove, IL: InterVarsity Press, 2008), 181–183.
6. Ellen G. White, *Prophets and Kings* (Mountain View, CA: Pacific Press, 1943), 508, 509.
7. See, e.g., Miller, *Daniel*, 123, 124; Christopher J. H. Wright, *Hearing the Message of Daniel: Sustaining Faith in Today's World* (Grand Rapids, MI: Zondervan, 2017), 85, 86.
8. Hector I. Avalos, "The Comedic Function of The Enumerations of Officials and Instruments in Daniel 3," *Catholic Biblical Quarterly* 53, no. 4 (October 1991): 580–588.
9. Ronald W. Pierce, *Daniel*, Teach the Text Commentary Series (Grand Rapids, MI: Baker Books, 2015), 50, 51.
10. John H Walton, ed., *Isaiah, Jeremiah, Lamentations, Ezekiel, Daniel*, Zondervan Illustrated Bible Backgrounds Commentary, vol. 4 (Grand Rapids, MI: Zondervan, 2009), 538.

11. Andrew E. Steinmann, *Daniel*, Concordia Commentary (Saint Louis, MO: Concordia Publishing, 2008), 186.

12. Pierce, *Daniel*, 55.

13. Robert Bartlett, *Why Can the Dead Do Such Great Things? Saints and Worshippers From the Martyrs to the Reformation* (Princeton, NJ: Princeton University Press, 2013), 379.

14. Leighton Ford, *Good News Is for Sharing* (Elgin, IL: David C. Cook, 1987), 16.

CHAPTER 5

From Pride to Humility

Nebuchadnezzar's presence in Daniel's narrative concludes with another dream, his banishment from the throne, and his eventual restoration to kingship. Together with chapter 5, chapter 4 composes the center of the Aramaic section by conveying God's judgment on proud rulers. For the sake of simplicity, chapter 4 can be broadly divided into three main sections in which the dream is told (verses 1–18), interpreted (verses 19–27), and fulfilled (verses 28–37). It is a personal letter from the king to all of his subjects, in which Nebuchadnezzar finally acknowledges God's power and authority over human affairs.

The dream is reported

Near the outset of his reign, Nebuchadnezzar dreamed of a statue comprised of various metals, of which he was the head of gold. Now, toward the end of his rulership, he has another dream in which he eats grass. Because he failed to heed the message of the first dream—to God alone belong wisdom, power, dominion, and glory—Nebuchadnezzar received the second dream, which came as an indictment for his failure to glorify God in all of his accomplishments.[1]

Like the first dream, the second dream also conveyed imagery familiar to the king. The king was shown a tree at the center of the earth, alluding to the cosmic tree, which was a common symbol of abundant life and well-being in the ancient world. As the tree grew taller, it reached the sky and became a shelter, providing protection and sustenance for people and animals.

A tree can be a symbol for persons or nations in the Old Testament. Ezekiel applied the metaphor of a cedar tree to Assyria and Egypt (Ezekiel 31). Moreover, in reaching to the sky, the tree evokes human hubris and reminds us of another project aimed at the sky—namely, the Tower of Babel (Genesis 11).

In its location at the center of the earth and in its visibility to the whole world, the tree represents the prominence of Babylon as a world empire. As one author notes, "The nations once 'scattered abroad upon the face of the whole earth' (Gen. 11.4, 8) with the subsequent confusion and fragmentation of languages (Gen. 11.7) are regathered into the harmonious empire of the king of Babylon. 'All peoples, nations and languages that dwell on the earth' (Dan. 4.1)."[2] Interestingly, the kingdom of God is also compared to a tree that grows and in whose branches the birds come and nest (Matthew 13:31, 32).

Up to this point, the imagery in its broad contours may not have looked mysterious to Nebuchadnezzar, fitting nicely with his perceived power and prosperity. Clearly, the height and opulence of the tree were beneficial to creation as it gave shelter and protection to all creatures. But what happens next sounded an ominous note to the king. A heavenly being came down from heaven to disrupt the idyllic image of security and prosperity. Daniel 4:13 refers to that divine agent as a "watcher" (*'ir*) or "holy one" (*qadish*). It has been noted that in "the Book of Daniel these two adjectives are used to describe a heavenly being that never sleeps and is always in the presence of the holy God. This is almost invariably taken by scholars as reference to an angel, although some consider these a special class of angels."[3] As the dream unfolds, the heavenly being commands that the tree be chopped down, bound with chains, and left in the company of the animals. This stump (Nebuchadnezzar) now eats grass, and its heart is changed from that of a man to that of a beast (verse 16).

How confusing the change of metaphors and images must have been to the king! Eventually, the dream concludes with the angel explaining the reason for these events:

> "This decision is by the decree of the watchers,
> And the sentence by the word of the holy ones,
> In order that the living may know
> That the Most High rules in the kingdom of men,
> Gives it to whomever He will,
> And sets over it the lowest of men" (verse 17).

Astonished by such a complex array of images, the king resorted to the wise men of Babylon, but no one could interpret the dream. Next, he summoned Daniel, who unsurprisingly produced the interpretation. But before moving on, keep in mind that Daniel 2, 4, and 5 go together because they contain stories in which Daniel outwits the other sages of Babylon. While chapter 5 presents the challenge of the writing on the wall, chapters 2 and 4 report Daniel's interpretation of dreams, again outsmarting the sages of Babylon. But unlike the dream of the statue, the king could remember the dream of the tree and did not threaten his advisors with death.

The dream is interpreted

As it turns out, the dream was bad news for Nebuchadnezzar. Daniel knew this and might have been tempted to deliver the harsh message with a feeling of revenge and satisfaction. After all, Nebuchadnezzar had subjugated his homeland, the land of Israel, to the Babylonian Empire. But this was not the case. Once Daniel realized the dream applied to the king, he was astonished. Though unafraid to break the bad news to the monarch, he was cautious and thoughtful. Characteristically, Daniel demonstrates sincerity and courage. His attitude is one of respect for the king, and he acts according to court etiquette, wishing the bad news of the dream to apply to the king's enemies.

Daniel then continues by intertwining the interpretation of the dream with the retelling of it. However, as one scholar notes:

> When he interprets the dream, he also omits some details, and their omission tells us something about Daniel. For the most part, Daniel works image by image through the dream as the king had told it (cf. 4:10–12 and 4:20–22; 4:13–15 and 4:23; 4:15–16 and 4:24). But when he gets to the worst part of the dream, he skips over the details. In the pronouncement of judgment, the angel had said, "Let his mind be changed from that of a man and let him be given the mind of an animal" (4:16), but Daniel does not repeat this part—nor does he interpret it. The text does not explain why Daniel skipped it, but perhaps he knew the king had gotten the point. He understood everything, and there was no good reason to say the most painful detail out loud. Daniel spared Nebuchadnezzar the last shred of his dignity—his humanity. The king's empire would survive, as the presence of the stump in the dream signified, but it would come at great personal cost.[4]

Daniel demonstrated his care for the king by what he said and what he refrained from saying. Unfortunately, we sometimes observe the misfortune of people we envy or dislike with perverse satisfaction. Yet Daniel found no satisfaction in the demise of the king. "Human suffering and misfortune, however deserved, should never be a cause for celebration or, worse, gloating."[5] Let us not forget what Jesus said: "Love your enemies and pray for those who persecute you" (Matthew 5:44, NASB).

Daniel's interpretation of the dream consisted of two distinct parts: the picture of a luxuriant tree, and its demise by the decree of the heavenly being. As for the tree, Daniel retells the dream with only minor differences from Nebuchadnezzar's version, applying it straight to the king: "It is you, O king" (Daniel 4:22). In the section about the messenger, Daniel omits certain details for reasons already noted and makes it clear that the ominous message was against the king himself. The king would be removed from the throne, banished from society, and forced to dwell with the beasts and eat grass. It has been suggested that such a condition seems compatible with a mania called *zoanthropy*, in which a person imagines himself or herself to be an animal and acts as such.[6] As the interpretation goes, such a condition would last for seven times—a temporal expression commonly understood to mean seven years.[7]

According to Daniel, the demise of the king would be temporary and would last until he knew that "the Most High rules in the kingdom of men, and gives it to whomever He chooses" (verse 25). Again, in the interpretation, Daniel reiterates that the purpose of the judgment is to make the king recognize God's sovereignty over kings and kingdoms.

After giving the explanation of the dream, Daniel acts in line with the prophets of the Old Testament. He makes a strong appeal for the king to break from his sins by showing mercy to the poor (verse 27; cf. Micah 6:8), which might cause the judgment to be postponed. Such neglect of the poor may be correlated with the king's failure to recognize God's sovereignty. After all, the one "who mocks the poor reproaches his Maker" (Proverbs 17:5).

Ironically, while Nebuchadnezzar described the tree as providing food for all under its branches, the tree actually did not provide for all because the king did not care for the poor in his realm.[8] A supreme function of a king in Old Testament times was to provide justice in his realm by protecting the downtrodden and the rights of widows, orphans, and the poor. In this regard, Nebuchadnezzar had failed miserably.

The dream is fulfilled

Twelve months after the dream, Nebuchadnezzar was walking about the royal palace and congratulating himself for building the "great Babylon" (Daniel 4:30). One commentator nicely summarizes the impressive and beautiful ancient Babylon:

> Babylon was a rectangularly shaped city surrounded by a broad and deep water-filled moat and then by an intricate system of double walls. The first double-wall system encompassed the main city. Its inner wall was twenty-one feet thick and reinforced with defense towers

> at sixty-foot intervals while the outer wall was eleven feet in width and also had watchtowers. Later Nebuchadnezzar added another defensive double-wall system (an outer wall twenty-five feet thick and an inner wall twenty-three feet thick) east of the Euphrates that ran the incredible distance of seventeen miles and was wide enough at the top for chariots to pass. The height of the walls is not known, but the Ishtar Gate was forty feet high, and the walls would have approximated this size. A forty-foot wall would have been a formidable barrier for enemy soldiers.[9]

At the very moment when the king was praising his supposed accomplishments, God's judgment fell upon him. He was removed from the throne and forced to spend seven years among the beasts, eating grass exactly as Daniel had predicted. When the allotted time of his judgment was completed, the king was restored to his former honor, but this time he finally recognized that "those who walk in pride He [God] is able to put down" (verse 37). Hence, the purpose of the judgment, as stated in each major section of the biblical narrative, is accomplished. Finally, Nebuchadnezzar comes to acknowledge that "the Most High rules in the kingdom of men, and gives it to whomever He chooses" (verse 25; cf. verses 34, 35).

Note that in Daniel 1–4, Nebuchadnezzar stands at "center stage in the drama that unfolds in his court. In chapter 2 his dream about the statue took down his incompetent wise men; in chapter 3 his garish image nearly took down Shadrach, Meshach, and Abednego; in chapter 4 his dream about the tree took him down."[10] Thus, with the fulfillment of the dream, the greatest ruler of the Neo-Babylonian Empire leaves the narrative of Daniel (as a protagonist) as he left history, when gold gave way to silver. He accomplished great military victories, ruled over many nations, and built a world empire but was helpless before the God of his captives. This reminds us that the Most High was, is, and will always be the Supreme Ruler over any human power.

From Pride to Humility

While Nebuchadnezzar had to eat grass with the beasts to learn humility, we are called to learn humility from the One who "humbled Himself and became obedient to the point of death, even the death of the cross" (Philippians 2:8). Maybe it is time to stop focusing on ourselves, our accomplishments, and our failures. Even better, why not stop comparing ourselves to others, their accomplishments, and their failures? Let us lift our eyes and look to Jesus who "has made us kings and priests to His God and Father, to Him be glory and dominion forever and ever. Amen" (Revelation 1:6).

Conclusion

In closing, a few points deserve further reflection. First, as God grants us greatness and power, He expects us to recognize His sovereignty. This story showcases one of Nebuchadnezzar's major flaws: his hubris and self-sufficiency. Since he appears to consider himself to be the center of the world, there is no room in his mind-set for his neighbor or for God. In such a worldview, God becomes irrelevant, and fellow humans are turned into tools for the aggrandizement of the empire. The purpose of the judgment predicted by the dream was to humble the king so that he would come to recognize the sovereignty of God over the world and the king's personal life. These observations provide an opportunity to reflect on the place of God in our lives. Are we able to recognize that all of our accomplishments in life are gifts from God to be credited to Him and used for His glory?

Second, it is God who establishes and removes kings. This is one of, if not the major, thrust of Daniel 4 and is reinforced by the parallelism with Daniel 5. These two chapters are the fulcrum of the Aramaic section of the book of Daniel, emphasizing God's sovereignty. "When we look earnestly at the person of God, we are compelled to honor and glorify him. This is why it is so important to keep the focus of our preaching and teaching on who God is and how he works with humanity. The former drives the latter, and we are recipients of both—even though we often come to know God through the way he works with mere mortals in Scripture."[11]

Third, God reverses judgment and restores sinners when they repent. His sovereignty is absolute but not arbitrary. As conveyed by the restoration of Nebuchadnezzar after seven years of ostracism, God remains ready to forgive and restore. Daniel's admonition to the king to amend his ways is an indication that judgment could be postponed or possibly averted, as was the case with Nineveh (Jonah 4). However, it should not be forgotten that God does not necessarily judge sin as we may want Him to. His judgment is much greater than ours because He sees life from a divine perspective.

> "For My thoughts are not your thoughts,
> Nor are your ways My ways," says the LORD.
> "For as the heavens are higher than the earth,
> So are My ways higher than your ways,
> And My thoughts than your thoughts" (Isaiah 55:8, 9).

God is eager to save, and we can rest in His infinite love and justice, knowing that He will solve the sin problem in a way that is consistent with His character.

---

1. Wendy L. Widder, *Daniel*, Story of God Bible Commentary (Grand Rapids, MI: Zondervan, 2016), 94.
2. Peter W. Coxon, "The Great Tree of Daniel 4," in *A Word in Season: Essays in Honour of William McKane*, ed. James D. Martin and Philip R. Davies, *Journal for the Study of the Old Testament* 42 (Sheffield, UK: JSOT Press, 1986), 92.
3. René Péter-Contesse and John Ellington, *A Handbook on the Book of Daniel*, UBS Helps for Translators (New York: United Bible Societies, 1994), 109.
4. Widder, *Daniel*, 95, 96.
5. Widder, *Daniel*, 99.
6. Ronald W. Pierce, *Daniel*, Teach the Text Commentary Series (Grand Rapids, MI: Baker Books, 2015), 78.
7. Francis D. Nichol, ed., *The Seventh-day Adventist Bible Commentary* (Washington, DC: Review and Herald®, 1977), 4:790.
8. Sharon Pace, *Daniel*, Smyth & Helwys Bible Commentary (Macon, GA: Smyth & Helwys, 2008), 134.
9. Stephen R. Miller, *Daniel*, New American Commentary, vol. 18 (Nashville, TN: Broadman and Holman, 1994), 140.
10. Widder, *Daniel*, 97.
11. Pierce, *Daniel*, 82.

CHAPTER 6

From Arrogance to Destruction

Daniel 5 reports events that took place in 539 B.C., when the Medo-Persian army took the city of Babylon. Although the Medo-Persian armies were just outside the walls of Babylon, Belshazzar chose to ignore the danger and threw a banquet with a thousand of his nobles. As the party sank into a drunken orgy, the king and his guests desecrated the Jerusalem temple's vessels by using them as drinking vessels while praising their manufactured gods. Amid the debauchery of the celebration, a hand writing on the wall of the palace announced judgment. That very night Belshazzar was slain, and the kingdom passed to the Medo-Persian Empire. This chapter shows the foolishness of Belshazzar's boastful arrogance and reiterates one of the fundamental theological points of the entire book of Daniel: it is God who sets up kings and removes them.

A feast and a message

Large banquets were common in the ancient world, but an intriguing element of the present story is the occasion for the massive celebration. Considering that Babylon was surrounded by the Medo-Persian army, one wonders what may have motivated the king to throw a party under such inappropriate and dangerous circumstances. A number of motivations have been hypothesized. The banquet may have been a celebration of the New Year festival of the moon god Sîn. It may have been a coronation feast for Belshazzar himself, given his father's defeat in a previous military campaign. It could have been a strategy to boost the morale of his people, given the adverse circumstances, or simply an attempt to live his last hours to the fullest since there was no escape from the enemy anyway.[1] Whatever the motivation, the party reveals a foolish and arrogant ruler, unable to understand reality and act accordingly.

In a demonstration of ultimate arrogance, the king commanded the vessels of Jerusalem's temple to be brought to the banquet to serve as drinking cups. Nebuchadnezzar had brought the vessels from Jerusalem and set them in the temple of his god, showing some measure of respect for the sacred objects. Belshazzar, however, rejected the most elementary principles of decorum in the ancient Near East, where desecration of "cult vessels was an outrage even by pagan standards."[2] And as if drinking wine from the vessels was not outrageous enough, the revelers also praised their gods while doing so. In the blasphemous use of the temple vessels, they likely intended to mock the God of Judah and show the superiority of the gods of Babylon.

At this point, it is important to highlight the significance of the temple vessels. One may surmise that due to the demise of the temple, the vessels housed in Babylon would have lost their status as sacred objects. It must be noted, however, that the temple vessels were metonymical objects that stood for the temple and reminded the exiled community of their linkage to the temple and the homeland. When the exiles returned to their land, they brought with them the temple vessels that Nebuchadnezzar had carried away to Babylon (Ezra 1:7–10; cf. Ezra 5:13–15; 6:5).[3] So Belshazzar's profanation of such vessels counted as an egregious sin and an act of outright defiance of the God of Israel.

Another point worth noting is that while the merrymakers drank from the holy vessels, they praised the worthless deities of gold, silver, bronze, iron, wood, and stone (Daniel 5:4). Ironically, they foolishly trusted in gods that were mere metal, wood, or stone, devoid of the power to act or save. Also, it is probably significant that the sequence and type of materials are exactly the same, except for the wood that replaced clay, as that of the image in Nebuchadnezzar's dream in Daniel 2. Such a connection may suggest that these gods will share the fate of the image, which was shattered by the advent of God's eternal kingdom (Daniel 2:35, 44, 45).

But God would not remain oblivious to the moral debauchery, debased worship, and profanation of the temple vessels. He considered such behavior as an attack on Himself. When the celebration was in full swing, and the king and his drunken guests praised their worthless gods, supernatural fingers began to write a cryptic message on the palace wall. Divine fingers appear elsewhere in Scripture to bring deliverance to God's people (Exodus 8:19), to write the Ten Commandments (Exodus 31:18; cf. Deuteronomy 9:10), and to create (Psalm 8:3). In Belshazzar's banquet, however, God's fingers bring judgment to an arrogant king and his kingdom.[4] "The God who creates, reveals, and redeems also judges."[5]

As the king contemplated the disembodied hand that was writing on the wall, he was terrified, and as the biblical narrative says, "the joints of his hips were loosened and his knees knocked against each other" (Daniel 5:6). Such language indicates that the king was overcome with panic, and the suggestion has been made that the king lost control of his bodily functions.[6] He had abused the temple vessels and manipulated the crowd, but when the ominous writing appeared on the wall, he was absolutely powerless. He invoked his magicians, but they failed to explain the supernatural writing. As a result of the commotion, the queen came to the palace and reminded the king of someone who could interpret the writing on the wall—namely, Daniel, a servant of his father Nebuchadnezzar. In this connection, two considerations are in order. First, the queen may have been the queen mother Nitocris, mentioned by Herodotus, the wife of Nabonidus and daughter of Nebuchadnezzar.[7] She seemingly speaks to Belshazzar with some degree of authority over him. The queen mother played an important role in many ancient Near Eastern cultures (cf. 1 Kings 15:13; Jeremiah 13:18).

It should also be noted that Belshazzar, although referred to as the son of Nebuchadnezzar (Daniel 5:2), was the biological eldest son of Nabonidus, with whom he was coregent. Therefore, the reference to Nebuchadnezzar as his "father" must be understood in the context of the ancient Near East, where "father/son" can refer to distant ancestors or descendants or unrelated predecessors or successors. In addition, the father-son connection becomes relevant as the narrative unfolds, inasmuch as it becomes clear that the son did not learn from the experience of the father. Moreover, while Nebuchadnezzar marks the beginning of the Exile, Belshazzar signals its end and the demise of the Babylonian Empire. Thus, although several kings ruled over Babylon, Daniel focuses only on the first and the last, drawing attention to the comparison with chapter 4 and alluding to Judah's seventy-year exile.[8] (For a list of the rulers of the Babylonian Empire and their presumed relationship with Nebuchadnezzar, see the table below.)

Rulers of the Babylonian Empire and their presumed relationship with Nebuchadnezzar

Nebuchadnezzar (605–562)	Mentioned 91 times in the Old Testament (most in Jeremiah 21–52; Daniel 1–5)
Amel-Marduk (562–560)	Son (2 Kings 25:27; Jeremiah 52:31)
Nergal-Sharezer (560–556)	Possible son-in-law; wife unknown (Jeremiah 39:3, 13)
Labashi-Marduk (556)	Possible maternal grandson (no biblical reference); murdered as a young boy
Nabonidus (556–539)	Perhaps son-in-law through daughter Nitocris (no biblical reference)
Belshazzar (550–539)	Perhaps maternal grandson (Daniel 5; 7; 8); also son of, and coregent with, Nabonidus

A few reflections may be appropriate as we draw some implications from the experience of Belshazzar. For example, it seems clear that profanation of what belongs to God is a direct challenge to His authority. This reminds us of how we should handle certain things that belong to Him, such as our resources, tithes, offerings, bodies, and affections. God claims authority over all of these things, and we should handle them as sacred vessels. We also learn from the story that God sometimes acts in a dramatic way to defeat human pride. Wealth and power may produce a false sense of security, but it evaporates in the presence of divine judgment.

A forgotten interpreter and a judgment

The pagan king's words to Daniel are noteworthy: "Are you that Daniel who is one of the captives from Judah, whom my father the king brought from Judah?" (Daniel 5:13). Such a patronizing address smacks of prejudice or racism. This mindset led Belshazzar to "forget" that the captive from Judah had served as one of the highest officers of Babylon and was a close advisor of Nebuchadnezzar. Prejudice, racism, and anti-Semitism appear whenever people forget that we have all been created in the image and likeness of God. Indeed, we are all brothers and sisters whose nationality is humanity.

Next, Daniel refuses the reward for his services, since such a huge reward might be understood as pressure to return a favorable interpretation. Besides, a reward would be useless in view of the impending demise of the king. Interestingly, after the interpretation is given, Daniel accepts the rewards since, at that point, the unfavorable interpretation would raise no suspicion of undue motivation.[9] Belshazzar offered Daniel the third position in the kingdom because Belshazzar was coregent with Nabonidus; hence, the third in rank was the highest offer the king could make.

But before giving the interpretation, Daniel offers a lengthy preamble, reminding the king of his own family history. The prophet recounts how God granted Nebuchadnezzar riches and power. But he became so arrogant and arbitrary that God removed him from the throne to topple his pride. Next, Daniel explains that Nebuchadnezzar repented, acknowledged God's sovereignty, and was restored. Finally, the prophet indicts Belshazzar, making it clear that the king has no excuse for not learning from Nebuchadnezzar's experience. Belshazzar's sins are the following: lack of humility, pride, exaltation against God, desecration of the temple vessels, idolatry, and failing to glorify God. At this point, it seems evident that the sins of the king are somehow related to the handwriting on the wall, which Daniel proceeds to interpret.

It must be mentioned that the consonantal Aramaic words on the wall could be vocalized either as nouns indicating weight measures or as passive participles. Daniel read the words as passive participles: *Mene* (mina or numbered), *tekel* (shekel or weighed), *upharsin* (plural of *peres*, half mina or divided). Thus, as Daniel himself stated: "This is the interpretation of each word. MENE: God has *numbered* your kingdom, and finished it; TEKEL: You have been *weighed* in the balances, and found wanting; PERES: Your kingdom has been *divided*, and given to the Medes and Persians" (verses 26–28; emphasis added).

None of the gods extolled and honored in the banquet could intervene and solve the ominous riddle. Ironically, it was the God whom Belshazzar despised and whose vessels he desecrated who provided the solution through one of the king's ignored exiles. In other words, the God deemed to be powerless manifested His power while the gods fabricated by human hands showed themselves to be worthless.[10]

As the narrative concludes, Daniel's interpretation is confirmed that very night. With the Babylonian leaders drunk, the Medo-Persians, who secretly diverted the Euphrates River, entered the city through the riverbed under the walls. Under the command of Darius the Mede, who was probably Cyrus's general, they overpowered the Babylonians and killed Belshazzar. Thus, the empire that captured Judah is itself captured.

Interestingly, Darius is the only person whose age is given in Daniel (sixty-two years), which implies that he was born about 601 B.C., at the height of Babylon's power and shortly after Daniel was taken to Babylon in 605 B.C. It follows from this that at the beginning of Israel's captivity, God was already at work to bring an end to the Exile, as announced by the prophets (Isaiah 44:24–45:8; Jeremiah 25:11, 12; 29:10; Ezekiel 34:11–16).[11]

At this point, some significant theological insights deserve consideration. First, we should note the expression "Spirit of the Holy God," which the queen recognized to be present in Daniel (Daniel 5:11). Although she may have used the phrase in a pagan sense, the phrase expresses the truth that the Holy Spirit empowered the life and ministry of Daniel in Babylon. Thus, the "excellent spirit, knowledge, understanding, interpreting dreams, solving riddles, and explaining enigmas" found in Daniel were gifts of the Holy Spirit (verse 12). But the good news is that God promises to give the Spirit abundantly to everyone. He not only enhances our natural gifts and abilities but also empowers us with supernatural gifts according to His purpose for our lives.

Second, but no less important, God wants us to learn from the past experiences of others. As we hear of how He worked with them, we can learn from their successes, failures, and challenges.[12] As one philosopher put it: "Those who cannot remember the past are condemned to repeat it."[13] It was precisely at this point that Belshazzar failed. Had he paid attention to Nebuchadnezzar's experience, he would have had a better grasp of God's character and how to serve Him. Besides, "the greater our privilege and understanding of God's ways in the past, the greater our accountability is in the present."[14] The more we reflect on how He has guided our forefathers in the faith, the more we will trust in the Lord and look to the future with hope. As Ellen G. White so aptly expressed: "We have nothing to fear for the future, except as we shall forget the way the Lord has led us, and his teaching in our past history. We are now a strong people, if we will put our trust in the Lord; for we are handling the mighty truths of the word of God. We have everything to be thankful for."[15]

Third, God's sovereignty, which at times expresses itself through judgment, stands as one of the most important theological points, if not *the* theological center, of the book. The present chapter shows God judging Belshazzar and making the transition of power from Babylon to Medo-Persia, begging the question, How does God's sovereignty make a difference in our lives? On the one hand, the conviction that God is sovereign should release us from the stress of having to fix the world. If we ever feel overburdened with the idea that our churches, families, societies, and workplaces depend on us for thriving or surviving, the biblical teaching that everything ultimately depends on God allows us to lay our burdens on Him. On the other hand, God's sovereignty does not excuse us from responsibility because His sovereignty leaves space for human freedom. Therefore, because God is sovereign, He can and does empower us for meaningful work and achievement.

It is wise to acknowledge and embrace the sovereignty of God, as illustrated from the life of a later monarch.

> Napoleon, at the height of his career, is reported to have given this cynical answer to someone who asked if God was on the side of France: "God is on the side that has the heaviest artillery." Then came the Battle of Waterloo, where Napoleon lost both the battle and his empire. Years later, in exile on the island of St. Helena, chastened and humbled, Napoleon is reported to have quoted the words of Thomas à Kempis: "Man proposes; God disposes." This is the lesson with which history confronts us all. God is able to work his sovereign will—despite man.[16]

Conclusion

Babylon evokes Babel—its ancient predecessor (Genesis 11). Both were icons of human hubris; both attempted to blur the line between heaven and earth; and in both stories, a confusion of language signaled the end of their projects. But the demise of the Babylonian Empire was not the end of the spirit of "Babylon." Babylon ideology reappears in Daniel 11 and with full force in the book of Revelation. Indeed, Belshazzar's desecration of the temple vessels was just a shadow of spiritual Babylon's assault on true worship and God's heavenly sanctuary. But like its historical counterparts, the end-time Babylon will eventually be obliterated by God's eternal kingdom (Revelation 14:8; 16:19; 17:5; 18:2, 10, 21).

1. Tremper Longman III, *Daniel*, NIV Application Commentary (Grand Rapids, MI: Zondervan, 1999), 136.

2. John J. Collins, *Daniel: A Commentary on the Book of Daniel*, Hermeneia (Minneapolis, MN: Fortress, 1994), 245.

3. Isaac Kalimi and James D. Purvis, "King Jehoiachin and the Vessels of the Lord's House in Biblical Literature," *Catholic Biblical Quarterly* 56, no. 3 (July 1994): 449–457.

4. Longman, *Daniel*, 138.

5. Wendy L. Widder, *Daniel*, Story of God Bible Commentary (Grand Rapids, MI: Zondervan, 2016), 117.

6. Al Wolters, "Untying the King's Knots: Physiology and Wordplay in Daniel 5," *Journal of Biblical Literature* 110, no. 1 (Spring 1991): 117–122.

7. Allen C. Myers, ed., *The Eerdmans Bible Dictionary* (Grand Rapids, MI: Eerdmans, 1987), 135.

8. Ronald W. Pierce, *Daniel*, Teach the Text Commentary Series (Grand Rapids, MI: Baker Books, 2015), 86.

9. Pierce, *Daniel*, 93.

10. John E. Goldingay, *Daniel*, Word Biblical Commentary, vol. 30 (Dallas: Word, 1998), 113.

11. Andrew E. Steinmann, *Daniel*, Concordia Commentary (Saint Louis, MO: Concordia Pub., 2008), 288.

12. Pierce, *Daniel*, 99.

13. George Santayana, *The Life of Reason; or, The Phases of Human Progress: Reason in Religion*, vol. 3, bk. 3 of *The Works of George Santayana*, ed. Marianne S. Wokeck and Martin A. Coleman (Cambridge, MA: MIT Press, 2011), 172.

14. Pierce, *Daniel*, 99.

15. Ellen G. White, *Selected Messages*, vol. 3 (Washington, DC: Review and Herald®, 1980), 162.

16. Michael P. Green, ed., *Illustrations for Biblical Preaching* (Grand Rapids, MI: Baker, 1989).

CHAPTER 7

From the Lions' Den to the Angel's Den

The deliverance of Daniel from the lions' den is among the most beloved stories of the Bible. From a literary perspective, it parallels the story of the deliverance of the three Hebrew worthies from the blazing furnace (Daniel 3). Both narratives show God's faithfulness by empowering His servants to remain steadfast amid the most harrowing trials. Both showcase captives challenging a royal decree and demonstrating their loyalty to God at the risk of their own lives. Both contain a divine messenger entering the fray to support and deliver them. And interestingly, just as Daniel's whereabouts are not known when his companions went through the fire, we are not told where his friends were when Daniel spent the night with the lions. But wherever they were, they would have, like Daniel, retained their integrity. After all, they relied on God, not on each other, to face life's predicaments.

The story implies that Daniel's integrity and loyalty to public service had the new king planning to appoint him over the whole kingdom, provoking the jealousy of Daniel's colleagues. Resorting to subterfuge, they crafted a scheme to get rid of him, only to have it blow up in their faces. As the narrative shows, God was with Daniel and vindicated him before his enemies and the king.

Daniel's experience models a lifestyle for God's people throughout the ages and shows that God remains faithful to His people. He may not deliver everyone from physical pain and death on this earth, but everyone will eventually be vindicated when the great controversy comes to a close.

Plot and accusation

Darius's administrative reorganization of the kingdom and his excellent public service set the stage for the narrative. The king sets in place an organization with administrative regions ruled by satraps and supervised by three presidents, including Daniel. But the structure, it should be noted, was established "so that the king would suffer no loss" (Daniel 6:2). This suggests that corruption was already a concern in those times. Hence, there was a need for a system of accountability, from satraps to the presidents, who would report to the king to prevent corruption and allow taxes and other funds to flow to the royal treasury. However, the issue that triggers the reaction of Daniel's colleagues was the king's plan to set Daniel over them. They could not take issue with Daniel's outstanding qualifications, but their jealousy, thirst for power, prejudice, and even greed turned them against him.

Unfortunately, true competence may not be welcome in some places, and faithful Christians may suffer because of their integrity. As with Joseph in Potiphar's house, it was his character and service that earned him oversight of his master's house. But his refusal to "sin against God" (Genesis 39:9) landed him in jail, where he experienced the blessing described in 1 Peter: "If you should suffer for righteousness' sake, you are blessed" (1 Peter 3:14).

Once Daniel's enemies decided to plot his demise, they put his life under a microscope. They "sought to find some charge against Daniel concerning the kingdom; but they could find no charge or fault, because he was faithful; nor was there any error or fault found in him" (Daniel 6:4). We are not told how the conspirators examined Daniel, but they must have closely watched his professional and public life, searching breaches of conduct, bribes, conflicts of interest, kickbacks, and dereliction of duty. They may have spied on his private affairs to find some reason to disqualify him from public service. But having investigated every corner of Daniel's life, they could come to only one conclusion: Daniel was uncompromisingly faithful to "the law of his God" (verse 5). As it turns out, their work did not require much effort because Daniel did not hide his faith.

Running out of options, they concocted a plan to pit the law of the state against the law of God. Under such circumstances, knowing that Daniel would side with God against the state, they could accuse him of treason and put him to death. The scheme to eliminate Daniel is clearly delineated in the following narrative.

> So these governors and satraps thronged before the king, and said thus to him: "King Darius, live forever! All the governors of the kingdom, the administrators and satraps, the counselors and advisors, have consulted together to establish a royal statute and to make a firm decree, that whoever petitions any god or man for thirty days, except you, O king, shall be cast into the den of lions. Now, O king, establish the decree and sign the writing, so that it cannot be changed, according to the law of the Medes and Persians, which does not alter." Therefore King Darius signed the written decree (verses 6–9).

It must be mentioned that such a decree seems odd in view of the fact that the Persians did not deify their kings, although they treated the king as the representative of the deity.[1] Thus, the decree should not be understood "as actually deifying the king but as designating him as the only legitimate representative of deity for the stated time."[2] That being the case, Darius would become the only mediator or priest between gods and humans. Such an idea—probably presented by the conspirators as a way to promote allegiance to him—may have been flattering to the king. But how often honey in the mouth disguises bitterness in the heart!

The conspirators presented the idea to the king in the name

of "all the governors" and officers. Such a consensus can hardly be achieved in politics, ancient or otherwise. It was unlikely that all 120 satraps scattered throughout an empire that extended from modern Iran to modern Turkey would have been consulted. Moreover, Daniel, one of the three presidents and the king's favorite, was not consulted. And most important, Daniel would have never supported a decree opposed to the first two commandments of the Decalogue. He treasured his heritage and would not deny the God of his fathers.

> "Yet I am the Lord your God
> Ever since the land of Egypt,
> And you shall know no God but Me;
> For there is no savior besides Me" (Hosea 13:4).

As with all laws or decrees, they are only effective if they stipulate the penalty for transgression. In this case, the instrument of punishment was the lions' den: "an underground cavity with a relatively small hole at the top that could be covered by a large stone."[3] In fact, fighting lions, either in forests or after letting them loose from cages where they were kept for that purpose, was an ancient sport.[4] Although there seems to be no other example of such a punishment during Persian times, earlier Assyrian texts refer to oath breakers being put into cages of wild animals to be publicly devoured.[5] Just the thought of being cast into a pit with hungry lions would have tremendous dissuasive power on any potential lawbreaker.

Thus, with a cunning strategy, Daniel's colleagues managed to convince the king to sign the proposed decree. To make matters worse, the decree could not be altered. They may have feared that the king would change his mind once he discovered the real intention behind the law, so they demanded the decree be made according to the unchangeable laws of the Medes and Persians. Esther 1:19 also mentions the unchangeable nature of such laws. And the Greek historian Diodorus relates the case of the Persian king Darius III, who regretted a death sentence he had mistakenly passed on a man. The king lamented not being able to change it because it was done by royal authority.[6] In the end, the king signed the unchangeable decree, undermining his best interests and ensuring the demise of his favorite officer.

At this point in the flow of history, Daniel was in his eighties, and the "excellent spirit" that was in him shows the work of God's Spirit in his life (Daniel 6:3). Place yourself in Daniel's shoes and imagine a hypothetical committee or government agency examining your public and private life. What would be uncovered? How would your finances and relationships hold up under scrutiny? Fortunately for Daniel, he had accepted the work of grace in his heart and had ordered his life after the letter and spirit of God's law.

Faithfulness and vindication

Once Daniel learned about the decree, several options presented themselves. He might have reasoned that if he were killed by the lions, he could no longer help his compatriots. He could have prayed to God through Darius, but this, of course, was unacceptable. He could have stopped praying for a month and resumed his prayer life after the decree was no longer in force. He could have prayed in secret in another room or simply closed the windows to avoid the prying eyes of his enemies. Or he could have offered silent prayers to God. But under the pressing circumstances, he decided to continue his daily practice of praise, prayer, and supplications in the open. After all, his "life of loyalty to God had been lived out in the open."[7] Anything less would be a concession to his enemies and a denial of his faith in God.

Daniel returned home and "in his upper room, with his windows open toward Jerusalem, he knelt down on his knees three times that day, and prayed and gave thanks before his God, as was his custom since early days" (verse 10). Praying three times a day reminds one of Psalm 55:17–19, where David prays "evening and morning and at noon" for deliverance. The custom of praying toward Jerusalem comes from Solomon's prayer of dedication for the temple. Solomon prayed that those taken into the land of their captors should face the holy city when they prayed (1 Kings 8:38, 48–50; Psalm 55:18); in heaven, God would hear their supplications and maintain their cause, forgive them, and give them compassion before their captors (1 Kings 8:48–50). Through King Darius, the promise of compassion was miraculously realized in Daniel's life.

The biblical narrative records the content of Daniel's prayer, and the text offers a couple of helpful details. First, Daniel knelt in prayer. Such prayer posture occurs only two other times in the entire Old Testament: on the occasion of Solomon's prayer at the dedication of the new temple (1 Kings 8:54; 2 Chronicles 6:13), and Ezra's great prayer of confession for national sin (Ezra 9:5). It could be that kneeling down may have been the posture associated with corporate prayers on behalf of the nation. Likewise, Daniel's kneeling posture suggests an intercessory prayer for the national sins of his people at a time when the Exile was coming to an end and repatriation was in sight. Moreover, Daniel's intercessory prayer, reported in Daniel 9, takes place in the first year of Darius's reign and further corroborates the view that Daniel's prayer may have addressed the spiritual condition of his people.[8]

As soon as the conspirators spotted Daniel offering his customary prayers, they rushed to the king with the treasonous news. In their accusation, they omit that Daniel was one of three presidents and instead refer to him as "that Daniel, who is one of the captives from Judah" (Daniel 6:13). Such phrasing smacks of prejudice, racism, and anti-Semitism. It recalls Belshazzar's patronizing address to Daniel as "one of the captives from Judah" (Daniel 5:13) and the Chaldeans' reference to Daniel's friends as "certain Jews" (Daniel 3:12). The probable insinuation was that a foreigner like Daniel could not be trusted; as an alien exile, he was not loyal to the king.[9] Such bigotry, racism, and prejudice are some of the most insidious consequences of sin. As one author notes, "Among the collective forms of sin that cast a blight over the world today are racism, nationalism, imperialism, ageism, and sexism."[10]

Darius had no option but to deliver Daniel to be cast into the lions' den. Entrapped by his own officers, the king reluctantly allowed the process to follow its course. Before sending Daniel to his presumed execution, the king expresses some hope that Daniel's God might save him (Daniel 6:16). In what must have been a painful moment for the king, a stone was put over the den's opening and sealed with the signet rings of the king and his nobles so that no one would attempt a rescue. After a sleepless night, the king comes for Daniel and calls out: "Daniel, servant of the living God, has your God, whom you serve continually, been able to deliver you from the lions?" (verse 20). In the Old Testament, the epithet "living God" always occurs in the mouth of His followers—Moses in Deuteronomy 5:26, Joshua in Joshua 3:10, David in 1 Samuel 17:26, and Hezekiah in 2 Kings 19:16—to refer to Israel's God as the true God, as opposed to the powerless deities of the nations.[11] It is striking that such an epithet for the God of Israel appears in the mouth of a pagan king. But in light of the supernatural rescue of Daniel, Darius had to acknowledge that the God of Daniel was, indeed, the "living God."

During that lonely night, the lions' den became an angel's den because God sent His angel to protect Daniel from the lions. Like the fourth man appeared in the midst of the fire with Daniel's friends, so the angel of God came to be with Daniel amid the lions. Angels play an increasingly prominent role in the prophetic section of Daniel, comforting the prophet and explaining the visions.

Daniel's deliverance was an act of judicial vindication: "My God sent His angel and shut the lions' mouths, so that they have not hurt me, because I was found innocent before Him; and also, O king, I have done no wrong before you" (Daniel 6:22).

Since the other side of justice is the punishment of the guilty, the king ordered the conspirators to be cast into the den of ravenous lions. The thought of punishing wives and children because of the sins of husbands and fathers goes against our most elementary sense of justice and is forbidden in Deuteronomy 24:16. Ezekiel 18:20 clearly states that the "son shall not bear the guilt of the father, nor the father bear the guilt of the son." But this penalty is consistent with what we know about ancient law. Though it does not mean that God necessarily approved of the king's actions, it is in "keeping with the prophetic promise that as Israel is saved, her oppressors will be turned upon themselves and be annihilated (Isa 41:11–12; 49:25–26)."[12]

Thus, the narrative that began with a decree forcing everyone to make petitions only to the king, concludes with a decree by the same king, commanding all nations to worship the God of Daniel. As one commentator has noted, the "inclusion of Darius' decree by Daniel the author allows him to summarize the lessons learned by pagan rulers throughout the narrative section of Daniel (chapters 1–6) before moving on to the section of the book that will relate his visions (chapters 7–12). The visions presuppose the actions and attributes of God set forth in the decrees of Nebuchadnezzar and Darius. The visions go on to relate how God will bring his eternal kingdom to his people and save them for eternity."[13]

From this, we learn that God is always worthy of worship and obedience, no matter the cost. But in order to develop Daniel's qualities of character, we must have a firm grasp of God's character as revealed in His Word. When circumstances arise that put our allegiance to the test, we can trust God to help us make the right choice.

Close reflection on the experience of Daniel could be a source of discouragement. The closer we look, the more we realize how far we are from such a high standard of spirituality. But fortunately, our task, the Christian's task, is not to mimic Daniel but to look to Jesus, surrendering all to the crucified Savior. Only then can we live more like Christ.

At this juncture, we should note a potentially unsettling spiritual lesson: the story of the lions' den shows that God is able to deliver us from our trials, but it does not guarantee that He will always do so. As one author observes, an "innocent and faithful Daniel faced hatred, suffering, and death, and God spared him. A perfectly innocent and always faithful Jesus faced demonic hatred, intense suffering, and an excruciating death—but God did not spare him. His own Son lived a better life than anyone ever had, and he died a worse death. Yet, whereas Daniel emerged alone from his would-be tomb, Jesus' emergence from his tomb guaranteed that we too will rise. Daniel may have modeled for us how to live, but Jesus, the greater Daniel, makes our living possible, worthwhile, and everlasting."[14]

Thus, the so-called prosperity gospel that promises health and wealth distorts the cruciform gospel of Jesus Christ. Jesus Himself has called us to bear the cross and follow Him. Many Christians have endured suffering and even martyrdom for the name of Jesus. Today, faithful Christians may lose their jobs, suffer persecution, or even die, in spite of their unwavering loyalty to God, but the story of the lions' den shows that God stands by His servants and will eventually vindicate His people and obliterate the opposing forces.

Conclusion

The story of Daniel in the lions' den concludes the narrative section of Daniel—although the Aramaic section continues through Daniel 7, which opens the prophetic-apocalyptic section of the book. Before proceeding to Daniel 7, it bears noting that there are some possible connections between the narrative and prophetic sections of the book and a few conceptual links between Daniel 6 and 7.

First, the conspiracy against Daniel illustrates the persecution of the saints of the Most High by the little horn. Second, if the laws of the Medes and Persians could not be changed, how much less could the laws of God? Yet, in a twist of irony, the little horn attempts to change God's eternal law, which the Medes and Persians would never have done to their own laws. And last, the presence of God's angel among the lions to protect Daniel anticipates the prominent role of angels in the second part of the book, possibly foreshadowing the role of Michael who rises to defend His people (Daniel 12).

Possible links between Daniel 6 and 7 lie in the examination of Daniel's life by his enemies. Their conclusion that his character was blameless certainly and ironically agrees with God's own assessment of His servant, as shown by His vindication of Daniel. As a result, Daniel's enemies received their due in the den of lions, illustrating the eschatological vindication of God's people and the obliteration of the little horn. This execution of the heavenly judgment in favor of the saints is the goal of judgment—the Son of man acts in their favor. As the king overthrew Daniel's enemies, so God destroys the little horn forever. With evil banished, faithful Daniel was restored to royal service. In like manner, the "greatness of the kingdoms under the whole heaven, shall be given to the people, the saints of the Most High" (Daniel 7:27).

---

1. John E. Goldingay, *Daniel*, Word Biblical Commentary, vol. 30 (Dallas: Word, 1998), 128.
2. John H. Walton, "The Decree of Darius the Mede in Daniel 6," *Journal of the Evangelical Theological Society* 31, no. 3 (1988): 280.
3. John H. Walton, ed., *Isaiah, Jeremiah, Lamentations, Ezekiel, Daniel*, Zondervan Illustrated Bible Backgrounds Commentary, vol. 4 (Grand Rapids, MI: Zondervan, 2009), 546.
4. See Ira M. Price, "Assurbanipal," in *A Dictionary of the Bible*, ed. James Hastings et al. (New York: Charles Scribner's Sons, 1937), 176.
5. John H. Walton, Victor H. Matthews, and Mark W. Chavalas, *The IVP Bible Background Commentary: Old Testament* (Downers Grove, IL: InterVarsity Press, 2000), Daniel 6:7.
6. Francis D. Nichol, ed., *The Seventh-day Adventist Bible Commentary* (Washington, DC: Review and Herald®, 1977), 4:812.
7. John C. Jeske, *Daniel*, People's Bible Commentary (Milwaukee, WI: Northwestern, 1985), 115.
8. I owe these insights to Wendy L. Widder, *Daniel*, Story of God Bible Commentary (Grand Rapids, MI: Zondervan, 2016), 133, 134.
9. Goldingay, *Daniel*, 132.
10. Walter A. Elwell, ed., *Evangelical Dictionary of Theology*, 2nd ed. (Grand Rapids, MI: Baker Academic, 2001), 1104.
11. Widder, *Daniel*, 135.
12. Goldingay, *Daniel*, 134.
13. Andrew E. Steinmann, *Daniel*, Concordia Commentary (Saint Louis, MO: Concordia Pub., 2008), 324.
14. Widder, *Daniel*, 145.

CHAPTER 8

From the Stormy Sea to the Clouds of Heaven

The stories of Daniel and his friends' faithfulness—their refusal to eat unclean foods, the deliverance from a blazing furnace, and the rescue from the lions' den—are well known and loved by people of all ages. Yet the accounts of strange creatures emerging from the sea, especially the horrifying beast with ten horns, might be a little much for children. Nevertheless, though Daniel 7 may not be a bedtime story we reach for, it is intensely interesting and relevant for our daily walk with God. The symbols and metaphors, rightly understood, make it clear that God triumphs over evil.

Previously, Daniel was an interpreter of dreams given to others. Now he is grappling with his own dreams and visions, needing angelic assistance to cope with the disturbing revelations. Chapter 7 continues the Aramaic section of Daniel and depicts a scene of four beasts, corresponding to the four metallic kingdoms of chapter 2. However, the distinctive genre and content of Daniel 7 are more closely related to the prophetic section of the book. Thus, chapter 7 functions as a hinge between the narrative and the prophetic sections, standing at the heart of the book of Daniel.

The vision dates to the first year of Belshazzar's reign, about 553 B.C., which was the first year of Belshazzar's coregency with his father, Nabonidus. At this time, the Babylonian Empire was weakening, and a new world power was looming on the horizon. God gave this vision to Daniel to encourage His people and show them that human history moves according to the plan of an omnipotent God. Monstrous and scary powers may attack and persecute God's people, but the heavenly tribunal will set all things right, and the Son of man and the saints will rule forever.

The four animals

In the vision of Daniel 7, the prophet saw four great beasts coming up from the churning "Great Sea" (verse 2). In Bible prophecy, water usually represents people and nations (Isaiah 17:12, 13; 57:20; Jeremiah 46:6–8; Revelation 17:15) and winds or storms symbolize war and conquest (Jeremiah 25:31–33; 49:36, 37; Zechariah 7:14; Revelation 7:1). These images help Daniel graphically portray the rise and fall of empires, as represented by the four successive beasts emerging from the sea. Since the Bible applies the phrase "Great Sea" to the Mediterranean, one view contends that these powers were Mediterranean kingdoms. This seems plausible since all the world powers represented in the vision are situated around, or even in, the Mediterranean Sea.[1] Another view takes the "Great Sea" as symbolic of the nations of the world or humanity in all ages with no reference to a specific body of water.[2]

Interestingly, some have suggested that the blowing winds and beasts emerging from the "Great Sea" to rule over the earth are a reversal of God's original purpose for creation. Instead of man or humanity (*'ādām*) ruling over the beasts (Genesis 1:26–28), the beasts are ruling over the earth. Additionally, all the beasts in this vision are composite creatures, expressing a violation of the natural order. But as the vision comes to a climax, the Son of man receives dominion to rule over creation, according to God's original plan.[3] It should be stressed that such views on the symbolism are not necessarily mutually exclusive, nor do they change the historical referents of the symbols.

As we study the prophetic symbols depicted in the vision, we should bear in mind that not all the symbols are explained by the angel, and "there is no interpretative comment on the first three animals, and no representation in the symbolic vision of the horn's punishment. There is more symbolism than interpretation and more interpretation than symbolism; each stands on its own as a revelation."[4] Thus, the parallelism with Daniel 2 becomes an indispensable aid in filling the gaps and completing the broad picture. The first three beasts are described as being "like" their animal counterparts (Daniel 7:4–6). The fourth beast, however, appears as the very entity it embodies.

Lion. A fitting depiction of the Babylonian Empire, which abounded in artistic representations of winged lions. The combination of the king of beasts with the king of the birds is an accurate description of the Babylonian Empire at the apex of its glory. A wingless lion conveys weakness and may symbolize the declining years of Babylon under the successors of Nebuchadnezzar. The lion receiving the heart of a man may symbolize either Nebuchadnezzar's humiliation and restoration (Daniel 4) or the settled king, enjoying the product of his conquests.

Bear. As a mountain dweller, the bear stands as a suitable representation of the Medo-Persian Empire. This empire originated in the mountainous areas of Media and the elevated plateau of Iran. This particular bear is lopsided because the balance of power between the Medes and the Persians tipped to the Persians. The three ribs can be identified with the three main conquests of the Medo-Persian Empire: Lydia, Babylon, and Egypt.

Leopard. The fierceness and swiftness of a four-winged leopard provide an apt symbol for the empire of Greece, enlarged by Alexander the Great. The four heads represent four generals who divided the kingdom among themselves after Alexander's death: Seleucus (Syria and Babylon), Lysimachus (Thrace and northwestern Asia Minor), Ptolemy I Soter (Egypt), and Cassander (Macedonia).[5]

Nondescript beast. This unparalleled beast represents the Roman Empire. From the conquest of Macedonia in 168 B.C. to the conquest of Egypt in 30 B.C., Rome's conquests quickly established it as the ruler of the ancient world. The iron teeth represent the destructive nature of this kingdom, reminiscent of the powerful iron legs of the image in Daniel 2. Thus, iron appears in connection with the fourth kingdom in both prophecies, identifying it as the same power in both visions.

Another characteristic of this beast is that it has ten horns. Since the angel explains that the ten horns are ten kings who come from this kingdom, the most plausible referents are the barbarian tribes that gradually took over Imperial Rome. Spreading out over the continent, theses tribes eventually evolved into the modern nations of Europe. This is one possible list of such tribes: Ostrogoths, Visigoths, Franks, Vandals, Suevi, Alemanni, Anglo-Saxons, Heruli, Lombards, and Burgundians.[6] Finally, the annihilation of the persecuting power comes with the observation that the other beasts had their lives extended for a period (Daniel 7:12). This most likely refers to the residual realms of power or influence left to each world empire after its dominion passed away.

The little horn

Although the previous world powers represented by the beasts described above were political in nature, the power symbolized by the little horn is different:

> "He shall speak pompous words against the Most High,
> Shall persecute the saints of the Most High,
> And shall intend to change times and law.
> Then the saints shall be given into his hand
> For a time and times and half a time" (verse 25).

This power performs three activities, which are religious in nature: (1) it speaks against God; (2) it persecutes the saints; and (3) it intends to change times and law, although only God can change times and seasons (Daniel 2:21).

At this point, the question emerges as to which power the little horn represents. A close look at history shows that the only power that fits the specifications is the papacy. At least eight lines of evidence have been adduced to corroborate this view.[7]

First, the horn originated from the fourth, or Roman, beast

(Daniel 7:8). But it is distinct from the Roman Empire, even though it shares some of Imperial Rome's attributes. Interestingly, the papacy adopted a number of titles and attributions associated with the Roman emperors.

Second, it emerges after the other ten horns were already established, indicating that the little horn emerged out of the decadent Roman Empire. History bears this out, showing that the papacy originated from the ruins of Rome. The power vacuum caused by the empire's expulsion of three barbarian tribes was filled by the bishop of Rome with the help of Justinian, who declared the bishop of Rome as the head of all churches and gave him certain civil powers.

Third, as the little horn ascended to power, three horns were plucked up before him. In the sixth century A.D., the Roman emperor, allied with the bishop of Rome, defeated the Ostrogoths, the Vandals, and the Visigoths—three Arian tribes that opposed the bishop of Rome.[8] This paved the way for the bishop of Rome to consolidate his power.

Fourth, this power became a persecuting power; this fact is acknowledged by the papacy itself, on the grounds that such acts are legitimate on the basis of the authority presumably granted to it by Christ.[9]

Fifth, this power attempted to change God's law. The papacy changed the fourth commandment from the seventh-day Sabbath to Sunday. Although this was a gradual and complex process, the Church of Rome eventually ratified the change on the grounds that it had the authority to do so. Moreover, the term *times* refers to human history and its succession of kings and kingdoms (Daniel 2:21). At the height of its power, the papacy also acted to promote or depose kings.

Sixth, this power speaks against the Most High, committing blasphemy. Some titles and attributions of the papacy—the priestly authority to forgive sins, excommunicate, and exclude individuals or groups of people from participation in spiritual things—clearly fall into the category of blasphemy against God.

Seventh, the link between the little horn of Daniel 7:8 and

the little horn of Daniel 8:9 shows that both symbols represent virtually the same power and perform the same actions described in Daniel 8:9: persecution and counterfeiting Christ's ministry in the heavenly sanctuary.

Eighth, note the duration of the persecution: "a time and times and half a time" (Daniel 7:25). The word *times* must be understood as dual, hence two times. The Aramaic word for "time" (*'iddān*) can also be translated as "year."[10] The Jewish lunar year was composed of twelve months of about 29.5 days each, bringing the year to 354 days. Every three years, an extra month was added to line up the lunar year with the solar year of 365 days. A prophetic year consists of twelve months of 30 days each, thus resulting in a year of 360 days.[11] Therefore, the three and a half years equal 1,260 prophetic days. This conclusion finds its definitive confirmation in the 1,260 symbolic days of Revelation 11:2, 3 and the forty-two months of Revelation 13:5. These time periods extend from A.D. 538 (the liberation of Rome from the control of the Ostrogoths and the decree of Justinian constituting the bishop of Rome as the head of all the churches) to the deposing of the pope in A.D. 1798.

The heavenly judgment

With the heavenly judgment, the vision reaches its climax. The initial focus on Earth and the rise of world powers now shifts to heaven. It must be clarified that the event described here is not the second coming of Jesus. Rather, it is an event that takes place in heaven, as the Son of man comes into the presence of the Ancient of Days. In the prophetic time line, this judgment begins after the actions undertaken by the little horn and prior to the second coming of Jesus, hence, the designation the *pre-Advent judgment.*

As the heavenly scene unfolds, books are opened, and a courtroom, presided over by one called "the Ancient of Days," begins its deliberations. Eventually, an eternal kingdom is granted to the Son of man. In view of such a majestic description of heavenly grandeur, the fleeting glory of earthly kingdoms pales in comparison to the one sitting on the fiery throne.

"No matter how high the human throne, this throne is higher. No matter how pompous or pernicious the human throne, this higher throne obliterates it with resplendent holy power. There is a higher throne, and it is occupied by a being who is thoroughly good, just, and righteous—a being who was on the throne in time past, is on the throne today, and will be on the throne forever. A being who will eventually judge all human thrones and reward the faithful."[12]

The first and central protagonist in the vision—the Ancient of Days—is described in terms of His personal appearance, His throne, and His surroundings[13] in the heavenly scene. This unique title of God occurs only in Daniel and evokes several biblical references to God's eternality (Isaiah 9:6; 40:28), contrasting Him with the fleeting nature of earthly kingdoms. Because He is clearly distinct from the Son of man, the Ancient of Days must be identified with God the Father.

No less important and equally central in the vision is the Son of man. He emerges as "an individual, eschatological, celestial being with messianic traits."[14] He is an individual because He is depicted as a leader of the holy ones. He is eschatological because He receives an "everlasting dominion" (Daniel 7:14). He is celestial because He comes with the clouds of heaven. His Messianic traits are shown by the fact that He has dominion and relates to the Ancient of Days in a special way.[15]

In the imagery of the vision, the Son of man comes to take the dominion that once belonged to the beasts. But while the beasts are evil entities arising from the sea, the Son of man is a heavenly being who comes with the clouds of heaven. In the Old Testament, Yahweh Himself rides on the clouds (Psalms 68:4; 104:3). Here, the Son of man emerges as a second power that shares the essence of the Ancient of Days yet remains a distinct figure. His relationship to the Ancient of Days evokes the Davidic covenant in which the king appears as the vicegerent (son) of Yahweh (Psalms 2:7; 110). This portrays the Son of man as a Messianic or Davidic king. Unsurprisingly, making a clear allusion to Daniel 7, Jesus repeatedly called Himself the "Son of Man" (Matthew 16:27; 25:31; 26:64; John 3:13;

6:62); this title also occurs in Revelation 1:13 and 14:14 and is one that best characterizes Jesus' relationship with the Father.

The nature of the judgment is conveyed by the clause "the court was seated, and the books were opened" (Daniel 7:10). This is a scene not unlike that of human courts; as the judge enters, the court is seated, and the facts and records of the case are examined. Because this judgment involves the examination of books, it has been appropriately called the "investigative judgment." The books mentioned in connection with the judgment are most likely records of some sort "in which the names and the deeds of men are registered."[16] Scripture mentions the "book of the living" (Psalm 69:28), a "book of remembrance" (Malachi 3:16; cf. Nehemiah 13:14; Psalm 56:8), and God's book (Exodus 32:32; Psalm 56:8). In addition, the imagery of the Son of man coming with the clouds of heaven is clearly linked with the high priest, surrounded by a cloud and incense, entering the Most Holy Place on the Day of Atonement.[17]

But the question emerges as to who is being judged. First, the judgment being "made in favor of the saints of the Most High" (Daniel 7:22) indicates that it must include the people of God. Indeed, one major purpose of this judgment is to review the decisions of those who professed to have accepted Christ, determining whether they will enter God's kingdom. Thus, when Christ comes, He comes to distribute His rewards (Matthew 16:27), which have been decided upon in this investigative judgment.[18]

Such an understanding of the judgment depicted in Daniel 7 is unique to Seventh-day Adventists. Most Christians have no room for an investigative judgment; they believe that upon death, a person is immediately judged and goes either to heaven or to hell. Therefore, a pre-Advent judgment to make such decisions makes little sense to them. The biblical testimony, however, clearly teaches an investigative judgment prior to the second coming of Christ.

As we reflect on this judgment, we may feel afraid and insecure about our salvation. In that regard, let us keep in mind that God has granted a powerful and compassionate Advocate to represent us in the heavenly tribunal—the Son of man. He has covered our sins with His blood and will stand for us in the heavenly court. Because we have been covered with the righteousness of Christ, this judgment is the vindication of our salvation. So instead of fearing the judgment, we should welcome it with joy and celebration.

Finally, the context of the judgment scene indicates that the little horn is also involved in the judgment. After all, the vindication of the saints of the Most High entails the condemnation of the power represented by the little horn.

> The primary purpose of the investigative pre-Advent judgment is the final confirmation of salvation and vindication of God's people (verse 22). But beyond the vindication of the saints and the condemnation of the little horn, the pre-Advent judgment also corroborates God's justice in His dealings with humanity. When the unfallen beings in the universe examine the records of the saints during the pre-Advent judgment, they will conclude that God has indeed been just and merciful in each case. In this way the character of God, which has been at the center of the great controversy between Christ and Satan, will be exonerated.[19]

Conclusion

The final scene of Daniel 7 portrays "the saints of the Most High" (verse 25) ruling forever in close association with the Son of man. God's eternal kingdom is established in both Daniel 2 and 7. Daniel 2 culminates with the kingdom of God filling the earth, and Daniel 7 describes the King who wins the victory over evil and establishes His eternal kingdom.

Truly, God fights the battles of the cosmic conflict alongside His people and supports them in times of spiritual challenges and suffering. When the heavenly court convenes, the judgment will be made in favor of God's people. In the end, when God's kingdom obliterates all the earthly kingdoms, we shall reign with the Lord "forever and ever" (Revelation 22:5)

1. William H. Shea, *Daniel 7–12*, Abundant Life Bible Amplifier (Nampa, ID: Pacific Press®, 1996), 25.

2. Francis D. Nichol, ed., *The Seventh-day Adventist Bible Commentary* (Washington, DC. Review and Herald®, 1977), 4:820.

3. Joyce G. Baldwin, *Daniel*, Tyndale Old Testament Commentaries, vol. 23 (Downers Grove, IL: InterVarsity Press, 1978), 159; John E. Goldingay, *Daniel*, Word Biblical Commentary, vol. 30 (Dallas: Word, 1998), 190; Robert R. Wilson, "Creation and New Creation: The Role of Creation Imagery in the Book of Daniel," in *God Who Creates: Essays in Honor of W. Sibley Towner*, ed. William P. Brown and S. Dean McBride Jr. (Grand Rapids, MI: Eerdmans, 2000), 190–203.

4. Goldingay, *Daniel*, 156.

5. Shea, *Daniel 7–12*, 93.

6. Shea, *Daniel 7–12*, 134–137.

7. Shea, *Daniel 7–12*, 137–142.

8. See William H. Shea, *Daniel: A Reader's Guide* (Nampa, ID: Pacific Press®, 2005), 116, 117.

9. For some sources, see Nichol, *Seventh-day Adventist Bible Commentary*, 4:831.

10. Francis Brown, Samuel Rolles Driver, and Charles Augustus Briggs, *Enhanced Brown-Driver-Briggs Hebrew and English Lexicon* (Oxford: Clarendon Press, 1977), 1105.

11. Cf. Jacques B. Doukhan, *Daniel: The Vision of the End* (Berrien Springs, MI: Andrews University Press, 1987), 21n41; Louis F. Hartman and Alexander A. Di Lella, *The Book of Daniel*, Anchor Yale Bible, vol. 23 (New Haven, CT: Yale University Press, 2008), 215.

12. Wendy L. Widder, *Daniel*, Story of God Bible Commentary (Grand Rapids, MI: Zondervan, 2016), 168.

13. Andrew E. Steinmann, *Daniel*, Concordia Commentary (Saint Louis, MO: Concordia Pub., 2008), 352.

14. Arthur J. Ferch, "The Apocalyptic Son of Man in Daniel 7" (PhD diss., Andrews University, 1979), 192.

15. Charles Lynn Aaron Jr., "Loosening a Knot: Theological Development in the Book of Daniel" (PhD diss., Union Theological Seminary, 1996), 102.

16. Ellen G. White, *The Great Controversy* (Mountain View, CA: Pacific Press®, 1911), 481.

17. Crispin H. T. Fletcher-Louis, "The High Priest as Divine Mediator in the Hebrew Bible: Dan 7:13 as a Test Case," Society of Biblical Literature Seminar Papers, vol. 36 (Atlanta, GA: Scholars Press, 1997), 161–193.

18. Shea, *Daniel 7–12*, 147.

19. Pfandl, *Daniel*, 72, 73.

CHAPTER 9

From Contamination to Purification

Although sharing common themes with Daniel 7, the vision of Daniel 8 employs distinct symbols and language. Unlike the unclean and wild beasts of Daniel 7, the vision of Daniel 8 features clean and domestic animals—a ram and a goat. Also, instead of the Aramaic language of the previous chapters, Hebrew is the language of this vision and remains so until the end of the book. This change of symbols and language is not accidental but appears to be an intentional strategy to reinforce the content of the vision. Indeed, the vision depicts an attack on the sanctuary and its subsequent purification on the Day of Atonement. Therefore, it fittingly employs symbols derived from the ritual service and uses sanctuary language. Moreover, it is worth noting that in the sanctuary ritual services, a ram and a goat appeared together only on the Day of Atonement. Thus, by its particular use of symbols and language, the vision focuses on the Day of Atonement.

Keep in mind that Daniel 8 recapitulates Daniel 7, adding new details and perspectives. Both visions complement and illuminate each other. The following discussion is divided into three main sections. First, there is a cursory examination of the conflict between the powers represented by the ram and the goat. Second, there is a review of the nature and activities of the little horn. And finally, there is a close look at the purification of the sanctuary depicted in the passage. This aspect of the Daniel 8 vision is the subject of Seventh-day Adventism's most distinctive belief.

The ram and the goat

This vision is linked with the vision of Daniel 7: "In the third year of the reign of King Belshazzar . . . after the one that appeared to me the first time" (Daniel 8:1). As the vision unfolds, Daniel finds himself in Susa, which later became the capital city of the Persian Empire. Unlike the vision in Daniel 7, this vision begins with Medo-Persia, indicating that Babylon was about to give way to a new world power. The description of the ram with two uneven horns parallels the lopsided bear of the previous vision (and the silver of Daniel 2). Interestingly, Belshazzar's third year can be dated to about 551 B.C., which is close to the time when Cyrus defeated Astyages, uniting the Medes and the Persians to eventually conquer Babylon. Likewise, the westward, northward, and southward advances of the ram correspond to the three ribs in the bear's mouth, representing three major conquests of the Medo-Persian Empire: Lydia, Babylon, and Egypt. In the interpretation, Gabriel clarifies that the two-horned ram represents the kings of Media and Persia (Daniel 8:20).

Next, a flying, single-horned goat (corresponding to the leopard of Daniel 7 and the bronze of Daniel 2) comes from the west, attacking and defeating the ram. At the height of its power, the large horn of the goat breaks off, and four horns grow in its place toward the four winds of heaven. Later, Gabriel identifies this goat with Greece, the big horn with its first king, and the four subsequent horns with four less powerful kingdoms that would emerge from it (Daniel 8:21, 22). History confirms with extraordinary precision the prophetic fulfillment of the symbolism shown in the vision. The flying goat aptly depicts the swift military advances and widespread nature of Alexander's conquests. He invaded the Persian Empire in 334 B.C. Following a series of major battles, he quickly defeated the armies of Persia, took control of the Mediterranean coast down to Egypt, and marched to the interior of Asia. In a period of about twelve years, Alexander had taken over the entire Persian realm, establishing "the greatest empire the Near East had known up to that time."[1] According to one source, Alexander's empire, at its largest, "was 2 million square miles" and "stretched from Greece all the way to India."[2]

As the prophecy predicted, he died at the height of his power, and the empire was divided among four of his generals. Cassander took over Macedonia, Lysimachus inherited Thrace and northwestern Asia Minor, Seleucus I Nicator established himself in Syria and Babylonia, and Ptolemy took possession of Egypt. Eventually, the Seleucids and the Ptolemies emerged as dominant and rival dynasties, whose military and political engagements appear in the prophecy of Daniel 11.

The little horn

As the vision comes to a climax, a little horn appears. It grows quickly, and after a horizontal expansion, it directs its attacks toward heaven. In order to understand the significance of this symbolism, we must ascertain its origins, identify its referent, and examine its activities.

Origins. One of the difficult issues regarding the little horn concerns its point of origin. The New King James Version captures the ambiguity of the original language well: "And out of one of them came a little horn which grew exceedingly great toward the south, toward the east, and toward the Glorious Land" (Daniel 8:9). Most commentators hold that the horn arose from one of the four horns, which would identify the horn with the generally held Antiochene view of the passage.

But closer study brings a more plausible view. The relevant sections of verses 8 and 9 read as follows: "In place of it [the big horn] four notable ones came up toward the four winds of heaven. And out of one of them came a little horn." The immediate antecedent of "out of one of them" shows that the "little horn" came from one of the four winds of heaven, as noted in the following table:[3]

Gender and number agreement in Daniel 8:8, 9

Verse 8	toward the four winds (fem.)	of heaven (masc.)
Verse 9	and out of one (fem.)	of them (masc.)

Thus, from the syntactic parallelism that matches the gender of the words, it becomes clear that the little horn must come from one of the four quadrants of the compass. An objection may be raised that a horn must grow from another horn or from an animal's head. But this can be explained in either of two ways. Zechariah depicts the powers that led God's people into exile as horns, which apparently stand by themselves (Zechariah 1:18–21), showing that a symbolic horn does not necessarily require attachment to a beast or even to another horn. Another plausible explanation posits that the horn was indeed attached to a beast, but it lay "outside of the frame of the vision, and thus Daniel does not see it."[4] It has been suggested that the reason for not mentioning "such a terrible beast is that the animals used to represent the kingdoms (ram and goat) are clean animals, while such a beast would have to be considered unclean. That would have distorted the connection between the vision and the sanctuary."[5]

Whatever explanation one adopts, it seems clear that the little horn of Daniel 8 corresponds to the one of Daniel 7, so if they are not identical, they must overlap considerably, as shown in this convenient summary: "1. Both horns are little in the beginning (Dan. 7:8; 8:9). 2. Both become great later on (Dan. 7:20; 8:9ff.). 3. Both are persecuting powers (Dan. 7:21, 25; 8:10, 24). 4. Both are self-exalting and blasphemous (Dan. 7:8, 20, 25; 8:10, 11, 25). 5. Both target God's people (Dan. 7:25; 8:24). 6. Both have aspects of their activity delineated by prophetic time (Dan. 7:25; 8:13, 14). 7. Both extend until the time of the end (Dan. 7:25, 26; 8:17, 19). 8. And both face supernatural destruction (Dan. 7:11, 26; 8:25)."[6] It follows from this that since the little horn of chapter 7 originated from the nondescript beast symbolizing pagan Rome, the little horn depicted in Daniel 8 must have originated from the same power.

Identification. Most evangelical scholars interpret the little horn as representing the Seleucid king Antiochus IV. This king invaded Judea and desecrated the temple by entering and plundering it. He imposed a ruthless Hellenization program with the intention of eradicating the Jewish religion. He forbade Sabbath observance and the festivals. He abolished the sacrificial system, stopped the circumcision of children, and ordered that copies of the Torah be destroyed. This began on December 16, 167 B.C., when a statue of Zeus was set up in the temple and swine were sacrificed. It ended in 164 B.C., when the Maccabees defeated Antiochus and rededicated the temple.[7]

Seventh-day Adventists, however, interpret the apocalyptic prophecies according to the historicist method and also take into account the exegetical and contextual aspects of the biblical text. We contend that the horn must point to the papacy—a power that incorporated elements of the Roman Empire. This view is consistent with the origins of the little horn. The little horn came from one of the four quadrants of the compass and holds a close identification with the horn of Daniel 7, as already noted. On these grounds alone, the Antiochene interpretation becomes much less plausible.

However, Seventh-day Adventists reject the Antiochene identification of the little horn for several other reasons, some of which are summarized in the following quotation:

> 1. The little horn came up among 10 horns (Dan. 7:8), but Antiochus IV did not emerge among 10 Hellenistic kings. He was the eighth king in the Seleucid kingdom, which had 28 kings during its existence. 2. The vision in Daniel has three horns plucked up before it (verse 8). Antiochus IV did not uproot three kings. 3. The little horn became greater than the other horns (verse 20). Clearly Antiochus IV was not greater than the other kings of his time. In fact, the presence of the Roman ambassador Popilius Laenas was sufficient to cause Antiochus IV to withdraw from Egypt. 4. The saints were given into his hands for three and a half times/years

> (verse 25). According to 1 Maccabees 1:57 and 4:52-54, the desecration of the Temple lasted only three years and 10 days. 5. The ram (Persia) became great (Dan. 8:4); the goat (Greece) grew very great (verse 8); and the little horn grew exceedingly great (verse 9). At no time was Antiochus IV greater than Medo-Persia or Greece.[8]

None of the features match Antiochus as well as they match the Roman power and the papacy.

Activities. A number of activities predicted for the little horn do not fit with the Antiochene view yet seem consistent with the activities of the Roman power in both its pagan and papal phases.

The relevant passages say that the little horn "grew exceedingly great toward the south, toward the east, and toward the Glorious Land" (Daniel 8:9). As the geographical movement indicates, the horn may come either from the north or from the west. Thus, the pagan Roman Empire fits well with this picture, as it came from the west to conquer Egypt (south), Syria (east), and the Holy Land.

Next, we observe that it "grew up to the host of heaven; and it cast down some of the host and some of the stars to the ground, and trampled them" (verse 10). From this point on, the vertical movement of the horn is described, bringing papal Rome into view. The stars and the host are not to be equated with literal heavenly bodies, angels, or pagan deities. In fact, the heavenly bodies symbolize God's people (verse 10). As Gabriel later explains, this power "shall destroy the mighty, and also the holy people" (verse 24). This is a fitting depiction of the persecutions, promoted by the papacy, against those who dared to disagree. The Crusades developed into attacks against certain Christians in the form of the persecution of the Albigenses and Waldenses. The Inquisition also spread persecution from Spain to Latin America, not to mention the massacre of the Huguenots on St. Bartholomew's Day.[9]

However, the power represented by the horn "exalted himself as high as the Prince of the host," took away the continuing intercession,[10] and cast down "the place of His sanctuary" (verse 11). At the height of its power, the horn launches a spiritual and theological attack against the "Prince." "Prince" stands for a Messianic figure and thus refers to Christ in His heavenly position,[11] subsequently designated as Michael (Daniel 10:13, 21; 12:1). The removal of the continuous intercession and the casting down of the sanctuary symbolize the establishment of a false worship system, carried out by the papacy. Thus, God's heavenly ministry becomes obliterated in the hearts of the multitudes attracted to Rome's counterfeit gospel. It is not an exaggeration to say that a number of papal innovations, such as auricular confession, the sacrifice of the Mass, and the cult of the saints, constituted an attack on Christ's heavenly ministry.

The purification and vindication of the sanctuary

After depicting the activities of the little horn, the prophet hears two heavenly beings speaking with one another:

> Then I heard a holy one speaking; and another holy one said to that certain one who was speaking, "How long will the vision be, concerning the daily sacrifices and the transgression of desolation, the giving of both the sanctuary and the host to be trampled underfoot?"
>
> And he said to me, "For two thousand three hundred days; then the sanctuary shall be cleansed" (Daniel 8:13, 14).

This statement about the purification of the sanctuary corresponds to the judgment scene described in Daniel 7. The word translated here as "cleansed" includes the notions of being vindicated and restored. Both visions, though using distinct symbols, refer to the same heavenly judgment, occurring in heaven after the "two thousand three hundred days." Therefore, the sanctuary at issue must be the heavenly one.

Another point worthy of attention relates to the question asked and answered by the two heavenly beings. The inquiry is not about the length of the persecution perpetrated by the little horn. Rather, it concerns the length of the entire vision, from the Persian ram to the purification of the sanctuary. In the question of how long the vision will last, the vision (*ḥāzōn*) applies to the long-range events shown to Daniel, which extend from the Persian ram to the purification of the sanctuary. The word *sacrifice* does not appear in Hebrew; it may be implied, but it does not limit the scope of the vision.

It becomes apparent that twenty-three hundred evenings and mornings will transpire before the sanctuary is purified. To understand this symbolism, one has to review the ritual system God established to illustrate the plan of salvation.

The services of the Israelite sanctuary took place in two phases: (1) a daily service in which the sins of God's people were daily transferred to the sanctuary through confession and sacrifice; and (2) a yearly service, called the Day of Atonement, when the sanctuary was purified from the sins that had been transferred to it during the daily service. The "Day of Atonement was a day of judgment (Lev. 23:29). The predominant aspect was the vindication of the faithful and loyal Israelites who had utilized all the provisions given by God to be restored during the daily services of the ritual year."[12] At the same time, through the rituals of the Day of Atonement, "YHWH's justice is vindicated, whether those who remain loyal are cleared or those who now eschew humility and obedience to him are condemned."[13]

The purification of the sanctuary, which corresponds to the pre-Advent investigative judgment described in Daniel 7:9–14, must take place at the end of the twenty-three hundred prophetic days. This purification consists of examining the records of the lives of the saints, as noted in the last chapter (Daniel 7:22). At its conclusion, either the names or the sins are blotted out. "Through this pre-Advent judgment the true plan of salvation is established and the scheme of the little horn is condemned. The spiritual conflict between the two systems is decided, and God is justified before the universe (Rom. 3:4). In other words, the pre-Advent judgment vindicates not only the saints but also God before all created beings, including Satan and his followers."[14]

It is important to keep in mind that in Daniel 7 and 8, the judgment or Day of Atonement also deals with the attacks of the horn against the sanctuary. Like the Israelite sanctuary and temple, which could be desecrated by enemy forces, the heavenly temple must be vindicated from the effects of the counterfeit plan of salvation established by the papacy, which symbolically defiled the sanctuary.

> Thus, there have been two rival plans of sanctuary ministry and salvation—the heavenly original and the earthly substitute. There have been two rival sanctuaries and two rival priesthoods. There have been two rival high priests who have officiated over these plans. At some point in the history of this struggle, there must come a time for a decision between these two plans and their results. There has to come a time of judgment that will decide between them. This judgment is what is brought to view in the time period of Daniel 8:14, the 2300 days. The "cleansing" (KJV) or "reconsecration" (NIV) of the sanctuary thus has to do with righting the wrongs that the little horn has created in its attempt to establish an earthly substitute for the work of the heavenly sanctuary. Through this judgment it will become evident that all during this struggle the true sanctuary was the one in heaven (cf. Hebrews 8:2). It will become evident that the true priesthood was the priesthood in which Jesus is involved in heaven (cf. Hebrews 8:1). It will become evident that the true services of the true sanctuary were those located in heaven with Christ, the priestly Prince.[15]

From the above, it follows that the period of the little horn's usurpation of Jesus' atoning work will end after twenty-three hundred prophetic days, when the sanctuary will be purified and vindicated. However, no information is provided about its beginning. At the end of the interpretation, Daniel was "astonished by the vision, but no one understood it" (Daniel 8:27).

The Hebrew word for "vision" translates *mār'ē* (appearance) and refers to the conversation that mentioned the twenty-three hundred days in Daniel 8:14. Daniel could not understand because no beginning point was given. Only later does Gabriel give Daniel this information, as shown in the discussion in Daniel 9:23–27. There we will learn that this long time period began in 457 B.C., leading up to the events of 1844.

Conclusion

Daniel 8 describes two major conflicts. The first contest consisted of a horizontal or military war involving a goat and a ram, symbolizing the clash between the Medo-Persian Empire and the Greek forces. In this war, the Greeks under Alexander the Great defeated the Medo-Persians.

The second war, however, primarily unfolds in a vertical way. The power symbolized by the horn launches an attack against the heavenly sanctuary and its "Prince" or High Priest. Indeed, Jesus Christ is the High Priest of that sanctuary whose theological foundations the papacy casts to the earth. In the gloomy scene of persecution, apostasy, and defeat, a message of hope emerges from a dialogue between the two heavenly beings: "For two thousand three hundred days; then the sanctuary shall be cleansed" (Daniel 8:14). As that long period of time comes to an end, the heavenly Day of Atonement begins. God's character is vindicated, and Christ vindicates His people, blotting out their sins from the heavenly records. The sanctuary message begins to be proclaimed to the world, and eventually, the power represented by the little horn "shall be broken without human means" (verse 25). Seventh-day Adventists believe that the twenty-three hundred prophetic days ended in 1844, at which time Christ moved from the Holy Place to the Most Holy Place of the heavenly sanctuary to perform His Day of Atonement ministry.

---

1. Gerhard Pfandl, *Daniel: The Seer of Babylon* (Hagerstown, MD: Review and Herald®, 2004), 63.
2. Debra Skelton and Pamela Dell, *Empire of Alexander the Great*, rev. ed., Great Empires of the Past (New York: Chelsea House, 2009), 51.

3. Gerhard F. Hasel, "The 'Little Horn,' the Heavenly Sanctuary, and the Time of the End: A Study of Daniel 8:9–14," in *Symposium on Daniel*, vol. 2, ed. Frank B. Holbrook, Daniel and Revelation Committee Series (Washington, DC: Biblical Research Institute, 1986), 389, 390.

4. Pfandl, *Daniel*, 78.

5. Ángel M. Rodríguez, *Future Glory: The 8 Greatest End-Time Prophecies in the Bible* (Hagerstown, MD: Review and Herald®, 2002), 50.

6. Pfandl, *Daniel*, 77; see also William H. Shea, "Unity of Daniel," in *Symposium on Daniel*, vol. 2, ed. Frank B. Holbrook, Daniel and Revelation Committee Series (Washington, DC: Biblical Research Institute, 1986), 187.

7. Michael A. Harbin, *The Promise and the Blessing: A Historical Survey of the Old and New Testaments* (Grand Rapids, MI: Zondervan, 2005), 365.

8. Pfandl, *Daniel*, 76.

9. See John Julius Norwich, *Absolute Monarchs: A History of the Papacy* (New York: Random House, 2011); Edward A. Ryan, "Spanish Inquisition," in *Encyclopaedia Britannica*, accessed May 17, 2019, https://www.britannica.com/topic/Spanish-Inquisition.

10. The Hebrew word *tāmîd*, translated as "daily" in some Bible versions, must be applied to a wide range of sanctuary services related to the first apartment, such as the burning of incense, the lamps, the daily sacrifices, and so on. Therefore, *tāmîd* is better understood as the continuing ministration of Christ applying the merits of His blood to blot out the sins of His people.

11. Pfandl, *Daniel*, 102.

12. Gerhard F. Hasel, "Divine Judgment," in *Handbook of Seventh-day Adventist Theology*, ed. Raoul Dederen (Hagerstown, MD: Review and Herald®, 2001), 840.

13. Roy E. Gane, *Cult and Character: Purification Offerings, Day of Atonement, and Theodicy* (Winona Lake, IN: Eisenbrauns, 2005), 323.

14. Pfandl, *Daniel*, 88.

15. William H. Shea, *Daniel 7–12*, Abundant Life Bible Amplifier (Nampa, ID: Pacific Press®, 1996), 110.

10

CHAPTER

From Confession to Consolation

The opening note of Daniel 9 differs from all other vision introductions in Daniel. The other opening formulas contain only the king's name and the year of his reign (Daniel 7:1; 8:1; 10:1). Chapter 9's introductory formula comes with the following information: chronological reference, "in the first year"; the king's name, "Darius"; his father, "the son of Ahasuerus"; his ethnic origins, "lineage of the Medes"; his title, "made king"; geographic domain of his power, "over the realm of the Chaldeans"; repetition of the chronological reference, "in the first year" (Daniel 9:1, 2).[1]

This detailed introduction signals that a new time has dawned for God's people because a new king has risen to power. But this monarch does not belong to the previous lineage of Babylonian kings. He is of Median descent and rules over the Chaldeans, which means that Babylon's grip over God's people has been broken. To emphasize that the time of captivity has expired, the reference to the "first year" of the new king occurs twice. This detailed introductory formula sets the stage for Daniel's corporate prayer of confession and the prophecy of the seventy weeks that comes as a response.

Another point to keep in mind is that Daniel 9 is thirteen years removed from Daniel 8. Yet the two chapters are theologically and literarily interconnected, illuminating each other. The prophecy about the seventy years of captivity spills over into the prophecy of the seventy weeks, which in turn is linked to the prophecy of the twenty-three hundred days.

Overall, Daniel 9 divides itself into two main parts: Daniel's prayer of confession, and Gabriel's message of consolation about God's long-range plan for His people.

Daniel's prayer

The book of Daniel portrays Daniel as a man of prayer, whose petitions elicit a divine response. But only two verbally expressed prayers are recorded, and interestingly enough, both involve the issue of understanding.[2] In the first prayer, Daniel praises God for the understanding and interpretation of Nebuchadnezzar's dream (Daniel 2:19–23). The second entreaty is much longer, framed with covenantal language and employs the exclusive Israelite divine name Yahweh (LORD), which only occurs here throughout the entire book of Daniel. It is a long prayer that occupies nearly two-thirds of the chapter.

After studying Jeremiah's prophecy, most likely Jeremiah 25:11, 12, and 29:10, Daniel understood that the seventy-year captivity was about to end. But he was still mystified by its relationship to the twenty-three hundred days of the previous vision. Of course, he had learned from Jeremiah that the duration of the Exile would extend for seventy years, meaning the captivity was due to expire soon. But the connection between the duration of the Exile and the twenty-three hundred prophetic days remained elusive. Would it mean that the captivity would be extended? Thus, with a heavy heart, Daniel offers a long prayer that unfolds along two main themes: confession (Daniel 9:4–14), and an appeal for mercy (verses 15–19).

Confession. Daniel opens the prayer with an invocation extolling Yahweh's greatness and faithfulness in keeping His covenant with those who love Him (verse 4). This provides a model for the prayers we offer today. They must acknowledge the greatness of God and be offered with full confidence in His promise to listen and respond accordingly. God's covenantal faithfulness stands in stark contrast to the infidelity of the captives that motivated Daniel's prayer. The prophet makes it clear that covenantal unfaithfulness on Israel's part was the sole cause of the Exile. But this is neither an intercessory prayer by a detached intercessor nor an individual prayer. Rather, it is a corporate confession in which the supplicant fully identifies himself with those in the wrong, joining them in their need of mercy and forgiveness.

Daniel's confession is specific and unfolds into two movements, listing the causes and the effects of the people's sins:[3]

Causes

A. Sin list (verse 5)
  B. Failure to listen (verse 6)
    C. God's character (verse 7a)
      D. Israel's character (verse 7b)
        E. Vocative address: "O YHWH!" (verse 8a)
      D.' Israel's character (verse 8b)
    C.' God's character (verse 9)
  B.' Failure to listen (verse 10)
A.' Sin list (verse 11a)

Effects

A. The punishment is poured out on Israel (verse 11c, d)
  B. God confirms the punishment (verses 12, 13a)
    C. Israel is guilty before God (verse 13c)
  B.' YHWH watches the punishment (verse 14a)
A.' God brought the punishment on Israel (verse 14b)

Daniel acknowledges the pervasive nature of Israel's rebellion and describes the sins of the people explicitly: we have sinned, committed iniquity, done wickedly, and rebelled. He recognizes that the people failed to listen to the prophets God sent, calling them back to the covenant. The failure was not limited to the leadership or to certain social classes but involved the kings, princes, fathers, and all the people of the land. Consequently, the Lord poured out on them the covenantal curses, scattering them among the nations (Deuteronomy 28). As the confessor admits the sins of his people, he stresses the contrast between God's character and the people's character: "To you, O Lord, belongs righteousness, but to us open shame" (Daniel 9:7a, ESV). Instead of blaming God or someone else, Daniel identifies with his people and takes full responsibility for their sins, acknowledging that they deserve every bit of the punishment they have received. Much like Israel, how often do we tend to blame God (or other people, for that matter) for our own sins and mistakes?

Appeal for mercy. After acknowledging that the people fully deserved the punishment for their sins, Daniel makes a passionate appeal for the Lord to intervene. His reference to the Exodus evokes the covenant, which prompted God's extraordinary intervention to deliver His people from Egypt, leading to the founding of the nation. Indeed, the return from the Exile will replicate the Exodus, as indicated by other prophets (Isaiah 40:3–5; Hosea 2:14, 15).

Consistent with God's character as revealed in the covenant, Daniel's appeal rests on God's merciful character, His reputation, and His honor. But of utmost importance for the purpose of this study, the appeal is for God to forgive the people and restore the place. Note that the phrase "Your people" occurs three times (Daniel 9:15, 16, 19), and references to Jerusalem and the sanctuary appear six times (verses 15–19). As for the references to the "desolate" sanctuary and the "desolations" of the people, these may echo the covenantal curses (verses 17, 18; cf. Leviticus 26:22, 31–35) and also evoke the appeal for mercy in the laments (Psalm 79:9; Lamentations 5:18). Variants of "desolate" or "desolations" occur elsewhere in Daniel in connection with the profanation of the sanctuary (Daniel 8:13; 9:26, 27; 11:31; 12:11).[4]

This brief overview shows that Daniel's fervent prayer concerns the forgiveness of the *people* and the restoration of the *city*, including the sanctuary. This central theme has major implications for the prophecy that follows.

God's response to Daniel's prayer

While Daniel was still praying, Gabriel came to visit him with an important revelation. A few observations may be helpful at this point. First, the reference to Gabriel as the one whom Daniel "had seen in the vision at the beginning" ties the present revelation to the vision of Daniel 8 (Daniel 9:21). The word *vision* refers to the appearance of the two heavenly beings and the twenty-three hundred prophetic days. Second, Gabriel came to make Daniel "understand the vision" (verse 23), which reverses the final statement of Daniel 8, according to which no one could understand the vision (Daniel 8:27). Third, the new revelation comes as a response to Daniel's prayer, in that it focuses on the two main concerns of the prayer—namely, the people and the city. Thus, Gabriel's message about the seventy weeks connects the dots between the twenty-three hundred days, the duration of the Exile, and Daniel's prayer.

The first statement highlights the twin foci of the message: "Seventy weeks are determined for your *people* and for your holy *city*" (Daniel 9:24; emphasis added). Seventy weeks equal 490 prophetic days (490 years according to the year-day principle). Multiplying the duration of the Exile by seven (7 x 70) leads up to Messiah the Prince. So, while the seventy years of exile are patterned after the sabbatical year, the seventy weeks (490 years) are based on the jubilee. The two periods are interrelated, and both time periods are patterned after the cultic calendar of ancient Israel.

It becomes clear that it would take seventy years to take Israel out of Babylon—a work entrusted to Cyrus as a human messiah. But taking Babylon out of Israel would take seven times longer (ten jubilees). It would be a work only a divine Messiah, the Son of God, could accomplish. "The 70 years (7 x 10) lead to the messiah of the sabbatical year, whereas the 70 weeks, or 'seventy sevens' (7 x 7 x 10), lead to a messiah of jubilee."[5]

To better understand what the Lord accomplishes for the people and the city, due consideration must be given to the time periods and the chronology of the prophecy mentioned in the next verse. In this verse, the starting point for the seventy-week prophecy is given: "From the going forth of the command to restore and build Jerusalem" (Daniel 9:25). Also, the fact that this long time period is "cut off" (verse 26) implies that it must have been cut from a longer period, contextually pointing to the twenty-three hundred days of Daniel 8:14. This being the case, both time periods begin at the same point in time. The mention of a "command" to rebuild Jerusalem indicates that the Exile would end shortly, and the city would be rebuilt. The command resets the prophetic clock and signals the beginning of the 490-year prophecy; the end of this prophecy will see significant events for the people and the city.

As for the "command" (*dābār*) to restore the city, we should note that the book of Ezra mentions three decrees dealing with the repatriation of the Jews: the first in the first year of Cyrus, about 537 B.C. (Ezra 1:1–4); the second in the reign of Darius I, soon after 520 B.C. (Ezra 6:1–12); and the third in the seventh year of Artaxerxes, 457 B.C. (Ezra 7:1–26).

Of these three, only the decree of Artaxerxes fully satisfies the conditions of this prophecy. First, it is the last and the most thorough decree. Second, it is the only one that mentions God's intervention, after which the language of the text shifts back to Hebrew, indicating that "the national restoration has indeed started."[6] Finally, as two evangelical scholars assert, "457 B.C., then, is the correct date to begin marking off the seventy sabbaticals because this 'word' to rebuild the city is associated with the return of Ezra and the reestablishing of the judiciary, central to the concept of a city (Ezra 7:25, 26)."[7]

Having established the beginning of the seventy-week period, we must examine its chronological features. From a general perspective, the text says:

> "That from the going forth of the command
> To restore and build Jerusalem
> Until Messiah the Prince,
> There shall be seven weeks and sixty-two weeks"
> (Daniel 9:25).

It has been suggested that the seven-week period (forty-nine years) most likely refers to the time related to the rebuilding of Jerusalem, spanning the years 457–408 B.C. This roughly corresponds to the time that passed between the prophetic ministries of Haggai, Zechariah, and Malachi to the close of the Old Testament canon. The "sixty-two weeks" that follow appear to be a time of silence,[8] leading up to A.D. 27—the year marked by Jesus' baptism and the beginning of His public ministry. In the climactic last week (A.D. 27–34), actions of ultimate relevance are carried out by the Messiah in favor of the people and the city (verse 24).

Of utmost significance is the fact that in the middle of the seventh week (A.D. 31) the Messiah is "cut"; this term comes from the language of the covenant. Making a covenant in ancient times included the cutting of the sacrifice into pieces, which coheres with the fact that the Messiah confirms the covenant and brings an end to the sacrificial system. The "cut" undoubtedly points to the death of Jesus on the cross and the new covenant established by His blood. Significantly, the immediate concerns of Daniel for the people and the city are addressed from a broader and universal perspective. Consider this outline of verse 24:

"Seventy weeks are determined [or cut off]"

"For your people"	"And for your holy city"
1. "To finish the transgression"	1. "To bring in everlasting righteousness"
2. "To make an end of sins"	2. "To seal up vision and prophecy"
3. "To make reconciliation for iniquity"	3. "And to anoint the Most Holy"

As shown above, three elements concern the people: "To finish the transgression, to make an end of sins, to make reconciliation for iniquity." This solves the side of the equation related to the people and nicely includes what Jesus accomplished on the cross, not only for the Jews but for every Gentile believer. Gabriel's revelation reflects a cosmic scope that transcends ethnicity and time, encompassing every person who believes in Jesus until the end of the world. The ultimate answer to Daniel's prayer goes much further than he could have envisioned.

On the other side of the equation are three elements closely associated with God's people. They also flow from what Jesus accomplished on the cross and relate more closely to the city, as seen in the structural arrangement of verse 24. As opposed to the human rulers who built "Zion with bloodshed and Jerusalem with violent injustice" (Micah 3:10, NASB), the Messiah will "bring in everlasting righteousness" (Daniel 9:24). Interestingly, the phrase "eternal righteousness" occurs as an eschatological blessing on Zion in a Qumran noncanonical psalm.[9] In fact, to establish righteousness stands as one of the most essential functions of the Messiah (Isaiah 11:4, 5), and in that sense, only Jesus can fill Zion "with justice and righteousness" (Isaiah 33:5; cf. Isaiah 32:1, 16; Revelation 21; 22).

The phrase "to seal up vision and prophecy" probably refers to the event involving the death of Stephen, understood to mark the end of the seventy weeks. The following reasons have been suggested to support this view: "(1) the group to whom Stephen gave his final speech—the Sanhedrin, the highest religious body in the land; (2) the form of his speech—a covenant lawsuit speech like those given by Old Testament prophets; (3) the prophetic nature of his experience at the time of his death when he looked up in vision into heaven itself; and (4) the fact that Paul's conversion has its roots in Stephen's death, so that Paul, the apostle to the Gentiles, takes the place of Stephen, the powerful preacher to Israel."[10]

While Jesus' crucifixion occurred in the middle of the seventieth week, Stephen's martyrdom took place at the end of the seventieth week, signaling the end of the seventy-week prophecy. In fact, as a chronological signpost, Stephen's martyrdom receives further corroboration from other unique features of his experience:

> The discourse of Stephen marked the transition of Christianity from the limits of Judaism to a universal religion,

> and his death marked the transition of the Church from a Jewish community to a world-wide fraternity. Said Alford, "Stephen, under accusation of blaspheming the earthly Temple, is granted a sight of the heavenly Temple; being cited before the Sadducaic high priest, who believed neither angel nor spirit, he is vouchsafed a vision of the heavenly High Priest, standing and ministering at the Throne, amidst the angels and just men made perfect." Augustine traced a parallel between the death of Stephen and that of Jesus; the charges the same, the condemnation the same, the prayers the same. Lyman Abbott suggested a contrast: Christ crucified, a lingering death; Stephen stoned, an almost immediate death; Christ was forsaken of His Father; Stephen with the glory of God and of his Lord and Saviour, radiant before Him; but whether paralleled or contrasted in circumstances with Jesus, he was like Him in character, and Christ so illuminated with His glory the whole personality of this first martyr of the Christian faith that His reflection still remains in the mirror of the world's memory.[11]

Finally, we must examine the phrase "to anoint the Most Holy" (Daniel 9:24). Elsewhere in the Bible, the expression *most holy* refers to the sanctuary or its vessels but never to a person. In the Old Testament, the sanctuary was anointed as part of the ceremony that initiated its services (Exodus 40). In this connection, it may be helpful to note that in addition to Daniel 9:24, the themes of expiation, anointing, and the Holy of Holies occurs only in Exodus 29:37; the context of this verse deals with the consecration of Aaron (the first high priest), his sons, the tabernacle of meeting, and the altar (Exodus 29:38–44).[12] Therefore, the phrase "to anoint the Most Holy" refers to the inauguration of the sanctuary, possibly involving the establishment of its priesthood. So the question emerges as to which sanctuary is referenced in the passage. Since Daniel 9:26 predicts the destruction of the earthly temple, the sanctuary to be anointed must be the heavenly one.[13] Thus, the anointing of the heavenly sanctuary takes place in the context of Christ's inauguration as our High Priest after His ascension (Hebrews 9:23–26). As a result of the heavenly anointing, the Holy Spirit descended upon the nascent church at Pentecost—evoking the Shekinah glory at the inauguration of the tabernacle.

Conclusion

From his study of Jeremiah, Daniel realized that the seventy years of captivity were due to expire, and the people would soon return to the homeland, rebuild the city, and restore the temple. But when he presented that situation to God in prayer, he received a much fuller revelation from the Lord. In fact, the seventy-year captivity seems to point to a much longer period of exile—seven times longer. It will take seventy prophetic weeks (490 years) for the people to receive salvation from sin and so experience a true return from captivity. Only under the terms of the new covenant will the broken relationship with the Lord be fully restored. Only then, through His sacrificial blood, will the Messiah finish the transgression and bring in everlasting righteousness, giving everyone access to the heavenly temple (Daniel 9:24).

What a privilege to live on this side of the cross and experience the fullness of what Daniel could only faintly glimpse. Through His sacrifice on the cross, Jesus freed us from the captivity of sin. As Ellen G. White notes:

> We have no righteousness of our own with which to meet the claims of the law of God. But Christ has made a way of escape for us. He lived on earth amid trials and temptations such as we have to meet. He lived a sinless life. He died for us, and now He offers to take our sins and give us His righteousness. If you give yourself to Him, and accept Him as your Saviour, then, sinful as your life may have been, for His sake you are accounted righteous. Christ's character stands in place of your character, and you are accepted before God just as if you had not sinned.[14]

---

1. Charles E. McLain, "Daniel's Prayer in Chapter 9," *Detroit Baptist Seminary Journal* 9 (Fall 2004): 265–301.

2. Paul Birch Petersen, "The Prayers of Daniel," *Journal of the Adventist Theological Society* 7, no. 1 (1996): 51–63.

3. McLain, "Daniel's Prayer in Chapter 9," 265–301.

4. Carol A. Newsom, *Daniel: A Commentary*, Old Testament Library (Louisville, KY: Westminster John Knox Press, 2014), 296, 297.

5. Jacques B. Doukhan, *Secrets of Daniel: Wisdom and Dreams of a Jewish Prince in Exile* (Hagerstown, MD: Review and Herald®, 2000), 140.

6. Doukhan, *Secrets of Daniel*, 143.

7. Peter J. Gentry and Stephen J. Wellum, *Kingdom Through Covenant: A Biblical-Theological Understanding of the Covenants* (Wheaton, IL: Crossway, 2012), 546.

8. See L. Stephen Cook, *On the Question of the "Cessation of Prophecy" in Ancient Judaism*, Texts and Studies in Ancient Judaism, vol. 145 (Tübingen, Germany: Mohr Siebeck, 2011).

9. See 11Q5 22.13, in Florentino García Martínez and Eibert J. C. Tigchelaar, eds., *The Dead Sea Scrolls*, Study ed., vol. 2 (Leiden, Netherlands: Brill, 1998), 1177.

10. William H. Shea, *Daniel 7–12*, Abundant Life Bible Amplifier (Nampa, ID: Pacific Press®, 1996), 69, 70.

11. Peter Ainslie, *Among the Gospels and the Acts* (Baltimore: Temple Seminary Press, 1908), 319, 320.

12. Doukhan, *Secrets of Daniel*, 153.

13. Interestingly, as the purification of the heavenly sanctuary is connected with the prophecy of the twenty-three hundred days, so the inauguration of the same sanctuary is related to the seventy-weeks prophecy.

14. Ellen G. White, *Steps to Christ* (Washington, DC: Review and Herald®, 1956), 62.

CHAPTER 11

From Battle to Victory

Daniel 10 draws back the curtain on the great controversy between good and evil. It shows that behind the veil of visible reality rages a cosmic and spiritual war that spills over into geopolitical conflict in Daniel 11. Though this chaos seems determined by the whims of human potentates, such conflict is simply the earthly manifestation of a cosmic battle between God and the forces of evil. Fortunately, the outcome of this cosmic war has been decided at Calvary, where Jesus dealt a mortal blow to the powers of darkness (Colossians 2:9–15; 1 Peter 3:18–22).

Before delving into the specific details of Daniel 10, we should note the following. First, this chapter functions as a prologue to the last prophecy, which predicts a great war, with cosmic implications, between the king of the north and the king of the south (Daniel 11–12:1–4). Eventually, the war culminates in the destruction of God's enemy (Daniel 11:45) and the rise of Michael (Daniel 12:1–4). An epilogue concludes the vision and the entire book (verses 5–13).

Second, the time of the last vision in the third year of Cyrus (Daniel 10:1) indicates that seventy literal years have elapsed since Nebuchadnezzar brought the first captives and temple vessels to Babylon in the third year of Jehoiakim (Daniel 1:1).

Whereas the first chronological note mentions a defeated king, the last one brings up a victorious ruler. Third, while the prophet could not understand the previous vision (Daniel 8:27), this one is understood by Daniel. This probably refers to the main thrust of the vision, affirming that God's people will be victorious.

As the chapter unfolds and sets the stage for the great warfare that follows, three interrelated subjects deserve consideration: the motivation for Daniel's spiritual mourning, the appearance of the Divine Warrior, and the great war announced to the prophet.

Spiritual mourning

The biblical text provides no information regarding the cause of Daniel's three weeks of mourning, but events taking place among the Jews in Jerusalem at that time may offer a hint. Given the decree made by Cyrus, a group of Jews had returned to the land. Under the leadership of Zerubbabel, they began to prepare the ground for the reconstruction of the temple. Soon after the altar was in place and the sacrifices had begun, the Samaritans offered their help. But because the Samaritans had a syncretistic religion, the Jews refused their assistance. They did not want to interact with people involved with idolatry and risk falling back into the sins that had caused their exile. As a result, a profound hostility arose between the Jews and the Samaritans.

Ezra 4:4, 5 summarizes the reaction of the Samaritans: "Then the people of the land tried to discourage the people of Judah. They troubled them in building and hired counselors against them to frustrate their purpose all the days of Cyrus king of Persia, even until the reign of Darius king of Persia." Lobbying at high levels in the Persian government, the counselors at the service of the Samaritans eventually succeeded in bringing the reconstruction work to a halt. Naturally, the people began to build houses for themselves, as recorded in the book of Haggai.

When Daniel learned about the situation in Jerusalem, he decided to take this dire problem to God in prayer. He mourned for three weeks, refusing food, wine, and anointing himself with oil (Daniel 10:3). In the ancient world, perfumed oils functioned as deodorant and also protected the skin in the dry and hot climate of the Middle East. In addition, anointing with oil was associated with gladness and feasting and so was not compatible with mourning.[1] By abstaining from choice food and lotions, Daniel shows that his personal comfort was less important than the welfare of his people. Likewise, by devoting a time to prayer while abstaining from the joys and pleasures so readily available in our consumerist society, we can identify ourselves with our brothers and sisters who can never experience such things. We are reminded that like our fellow believers under persecution, we are engaged in a cosmic battle, and this world is not our final home.[2]

Though not a total fast, Daniel fasted for twenty-one days. This period of mourning took place in the first month of the year and included the time of the Passover and the Feast of the Unleavened Bread (on the fourteenth and the twenty-first of Nisan, respectively). That "no meat or wine came into my mouth" (verse 3) may be an indication that Daniel had not eaten the lamb nor drank the four cups of wine required by the Passover ritual. Jewish commentators defend Daniel's decision with the argument that "the interruption of the Temple's construction justified his response."[3]

At this point, Daniel had spent about seventy years in Babylon. Many changes had taken place during that long period of time. Cyrus had risen to power, and thousands of Jewish exiles had already returned to the homeland. So the question arises, Why was Daniel still in Babylon? Why did he not return with the others to help rebuild Jerusalem? At least two possibilities can be suggested: Daniel may have considered himself too old for the long trip, or he may have decided to stay behind, closer to the seat of power and any opportunity that might present itself to help his people. Whatever the case, Daniel remained as committed as he was seventy years earlier when he arrived as a young exile in Babylon. More importantly, God remained committed to Daniel and answered his prayers. In this final vision, God made it clear that in the great controversy between good and evil, He will bring ultimate victory to His people.[4]

Divine Warrior

Daniel 10 finds the prophet Daniel standing on the bank of the Tigris. Lifting up his eyes, he sees an individual of dazzling splendor, probably standing above the waters (cf. Daniel 12:6). This may be the same being who commands Gabriel in Daniel 8:16, and from the description that follows, it is no wonder that Daniel was overwhelmed with fear and needed to be revived three times.

In regard to the heavenly being, seven features are mentioned: (1) clothed in linen, (2) waist girded with gold, (3) body like beryl, (4) face like lightning, (5) eyes like torches of fire, (6) arms and feet like bronze, (7) and "the sound of his words like the voice of a multitude" (Daniel 10:4–6).

Significantly, the combination of images and concepts conveyed by this description points to a figure of the highest rank. As used elsewhere in Scripture, linen symbolizes purity and reminds us of the priestly garments. Gold was often associated with royalty; beryl was a gem in the priestly breastplate; lightning appears in connection with theophanies; fire flows from God's throne; bronze reminds us of tabernacle and temple materials and warfare instruments;[5] and the voice of a multitude evokes the tumult of battle.[6] This description seems to portray a divine figure endowed with priestly and royal attributes, along with attendant military overtones. It is important to note that this "man clothed in linen" appears later in the book and reveals a knowledge of the future that transcends that of the other angels (Daniel 12:6), and he also takes a divine oath (verse 7).[7]

In addition, parallels between the above description and other biblical accounts of divine manifestations suggest that this heavenly being holds first rank among other heavenly beings. He may well be the same heavenly being that appeared to Joshua as the "Commander of the LORD's army" (Joshua 5:15). Later, He appeared to Paul on the Damascus road, where only Paul could see the vision, while his companions only felt the effects of it (Acts 9:1–9). But the closest linguistic and conceptual parallels are found in two other passages. Ezekiel

1:26–28 uses similar imagery to represent the radiance emanating from God's throne, and Revelation 1:12–16 employs like terms and imagery to portray Christ.

From the above, it follows that the glorious person who appeared in the vision must be identified with Michael, the Messiah, the Prince of the host, the Son of man, the fourth Man in the furnace of blazing fire, and the Commander of God's army. Therefore, He must be no other than the preincarnate Christ, who portrays Himself in the vision as a priest, king, and warrior. This is most significant in the context of the "great war" (Daniel 10:1, NIV) and the revelation that Daniel is about to receive. Indeed, the "reality of God's blazingly glorious holiness is an important truth to remember in times of trial and persecution."[8] When we feel discouraged and see no way forward, we are reminded that an invincible and glorious God stands by our side. As the angel (presumably Gabriel) subsequently informs the prophet, the future will be fraught with spiritual and geopolitical battles that will bring suffering to God's people (Daniel 11). But the "man clothed in linen" will bring us victory.

Heavenly warfare

Overwhelmed by the vision of the glorious, preincarnate Christ, Daniel had to be reanimated three times by a second heavenly being (Daniel 10:10). Rushing from heaven to help the old prophet, Gabriel[9] came not only to show the backstage of the present conflict of the Jews but also to reveal that God's people would be involved in a cosmic war many years in the future (verse 14)—a war that would be waged in both geopolitical and spiritual realms.

During the twenty-one days in which Daniel had been praying, Gabriel had been fighting against the "prince of the kingdom of Persia" (verse 13). On a human level, the battle transpired both in Jerusalem and in the court of the Persian king. In Jerusalem, opposition and danger threatened and discouraged the returnees; in the Persian court, the enemies of God's people sought frenetically to persuade Cyrus to stop the reconstruction of the temple. Indeed, it was a terrible time for the Jews. The glorious promises announced by the prophets remained unfulfilled and unlikely to be realized in the near future.

But as Gabriel lifts the curtain, we learn that the war on the human level is the manifestation of a spiritual and cosmic war—a war triggered by the powers of darkness opposing God's plan for His people. Gabriel mentions the "prince of the kingdom of Persia," who resisted him for twenty-one days, and Michael, "one of the chief princes," who came to help Gabriel in that decisive battle (verse 13).

At this point, we need to identify clearly the two opposing sides in the war. First, who is the "prince of the kingdom of Persia"? One scholar contends that this figure is the human king of Persia because "neither Satan nor any of his angels were a prince in the kingdom of Persia."[10] Likewise, another commentator contends that "*Cyrus* alone was the *prince of Persia*."[11] However, close attention to the text reveals several reasons that seem to teach otherwise: Gabriel could not have been detained by an earthly ruler; the term *prince* (*śār*) also occurs elsewhere in reference to supernatural beings (Joshua 5:14; Daniel 8:11); and the contrast and opposition between the prince of Persia and Michael suggests that the former must be a supernatural entity. As one commentator suggests, "Inasmuch as Michael is declared to be the 'prince [*śar*] which standeth for the children of thy people' (ch. 12:1), it does not seem unreasonable that the 'prince of the kingdom of Persia' would be a self-styled 'guardian angel' for that country from among the hosts of the adversary."[12] He must be one of the spiritual forces elsewhere referred to in Scripture as "rulers of the darkness" and "spiritual hosts of wickedness" (Ephesians 6:12).

Apparently, the prince of Persia refers to the supernatural, satanic power acting behind the scenes to influence the Persian king to thwart God's plan for the Jewish people. Such a scenario is not unique to Daniel. Isaiah applies the title "king of Babylon" to a supernatural, evil power that stands behind the historical king of Babylon (Isaiah 14:3–21). Similarly, Ezekiel mentions the prince of Tyre in reference to the human ruler of that city (Ezekiel 28:1–10), while applying the term *king* to the supernatural, evil entity that stands behind the historical prince of Tyre (verses 11–19).[13]

Second, who is Michael, and in what sense is He "one of the chief princes" (Daniel 10:13)? The proper name *Michael,* in reference to a supernatural being, appears three times in Daniel (Daniel 10:13, 21; 12:1) and twice elsewhere in the Bible (Jude 9; Revelation 12:7). *Michael* means "who is like God"; this interjection generally is used in connection with war (Exodus 15:11; Deuteronomy 33:29; Isaiah 36:20).[14] Given the context, the "man clothed in linen" must be identified with Michael—a fitting image and designation for the warfare context reflected in Daniel 10.

But if Michael refers to the preincarnate Christ and is fully God, the affirmation that He is "one of the chief princes" needs an explanation. Indeed, a couple of suggestions have been advanced to demonstrate that the expression does not reduce Christ's status.

One scholar suggests that the expression reflects "the divine plurality found in the early chapters of Genesis such as 'Let *us* make man in *our* image' (Gen 1:26), 'the man has become like one of *us*' (Gen 3:22), and glimpsed also in the mysterious figure of the 'Angel of the Lord,' in whom God is both the sender and the sent (Exod 3:2-6; Exod 23:20-25)."[15] If so, the "chief princes" would refer to the divine personalities within the Godhead.

Another scholar argues that the word *one* (*'aḥad*) in "one of the chief [*rīšōnîm*] princes" means "first" and may be translated as "the first of the first princes." This expression "is the equivalent of the expression 'Prince of princes' of Daniel 8:25 and refers, therefore, to the same supernatural figure."[16]

From the above, it becomes clear that a cosmic and spiritual battle between good and evil rages behind the scenes of human war and conflict. As Ellen G. White explains, "While Satan was striving to influence the highest powers in the kingdom of Medo-Persia to show disfavor to God's people, angels worked in behalf of the exiles. The controversy was one in which all heaven was interested. Through the prophet Daniel we are given a glimpse of this mighty struggle between the forces of good and the forces of evil."[17] Despite the ferocious opposition, "all that heaven could do in behalf of the people of God was done. The victory was finally gained; the forces of the enemy were held in check all the days of Cyrus, and all the days of his son Cambyses, who reigned about seven and a half years."[18] The victory of Michael over the prince of Persia stands as a token of Michael's ultimate triumph over the forces of darkness at the end of the great war described in Daniel 11.

Conclusion

Daniel's humble prayer opens a window on an invisible world where a cosmic battle unfolds between the forces of good and the forces of evil. But in the tumult of the raging conflict, Michael our Prince stands ready to help us. He stands up for us and will eventually destroy Satan and put an end to the cosmic war. Until the day arrives when "death gives way to victory,"[19] we can hold fast to the assurance that Christ has so graciously given. We have a Priest-King and Divine Warrior who fights our battles at every level. So let us take our burdens to Him in prayer, and let His sovereign and loving will decide what is best for us. The words of Ellen G. White are reassuring: "God never leads His children otherwise than they would choose to be led, if they could see the end from the beginning, and discern the glory of the purpose which they are fulfilling as co-workers with Him."[20]

When that glorious day arrives, and we behold "the man clothed in linen," the "things hard to be understood will then find explanation. The mysteries of grace will unfold before us. Where our finite minds discovered only confusion and broken promises, we shall see the most perfect and beautiful harmony. We shall know that infinite love ordered the experiences that seemed most trying. As we realize the tender care of Him who makes all things work together for our good, we shall rejoice with joy unspeakable and full of glory."[21]

---

1. John H. Walton, ed., *Isaiah, Jeremiah, Lamentations, Ezekiel, Daniel*, Zondervan Illustrated Bible Backgrounds Commentary, vol. 4 (Grand Rapids, MI: Zondervan, 2009), 560.

2. Iain M. Duguid, *Daniel*, Reformed Expository Commentary (Phillipsburg, NJ: P & R, 2008), 179, 180.

3. Jacques B. Doukhan, *Secrets of Daniel: Wisdom and Dreams of a Jewish Prince in Exile* (Hagerstown, MD: Review and Herald®, 2000), 158.

4. Some students of Daniel contend that Daniel 10 features only one heavenly being, who can be identified either as an angel of high rank (Duguid, *Daniel*, 180, 181) or Christ Himself (Edward J. Young, *The Prophecy of Daniel: A Commentary* [Grand Rapids, MI: Eerdmans, 1980], 227). Other commentators, however, see two different figures in the chapter, the glorious being in verses 5, 6 and a separate angelic messenger who appears in verse 10 to give Daniel the message (Stephen R. Miller, *Daniel*, New American Commentary, vol. 18 [Nashville, TN: Broadman and Holman, 1994], 281, 282; Francis D. Nichol, ed., *The Seventh-day Adventist Bible Commentary* [Washington, DC: Review and Herald®, 1977], 4:858). Although the text is difficult and the distinctions are not always clear, the latter view seems more consistent with the context and with the view that Michael is equated with the preincarnate Christ, as noted in due course.

5. Leland Ryken et al., ed., *Dictionary of Biblical Imagery* (Downers Grove, IL: InterVarsity Press, 2000), 124.

6. Andrew E. Steinmann, *Daniel*, Concordia Commentary (Saint Louis, MO: Concordia, 2008), 491.

7. Miller, *Daniel*, 282.

8. Duguid, *Daniel*, 182.

9. Nichol, *Seventh-day Adventist Bible Commentary*, 4:858, identifies this heavenly being as Gabriel. See also John E. Goldingay, *Daniel*, Word Biblical Commentary, vol. 30 (Dallas: Word, 1998), 291.

10. William H. Shea, *Daniel 7–12*, Abundant Life Bible Amplifier (Nampa, ID: Pacific Press®, 1996), 175; Tim Meadowcroft, "Who Are the Princes of Persia and Greece (Daniel 10)? Pointers Towards the Danielic Vision of Earth and Heaven," *Journal for the Study of the Old Testament* 29, no. 1 (2004): 99–113.

11. Adam Clarke, *The Holy Bible, With a Commentary and Critical Notes*, new ed. (Bellingham, WA: Faithlife, 2014), 4:608; emphasis in the original.

12. Nichol, *Seventh-day Adventist Bible Commentary*, 4:859.

13. For Isaiah 12 and Ezekiel 28, see José M. Bertolucci, "The Son of the Morning and the Guardian Cherub in the Context of the Controversy Between Good and Evil" (ThD diss., Andrews University, 1985).

14. Jacques B. Doukhan, *Daniel: The Vision of the End* (Berrien Springs, MI: Andrews University Press, 1987), 100.

15. Lewis O. Anderson, "The Michael Figure in the Book of Daniel" (PhD diss., Andrews University, 1997), 168; emphasis in the original.

16. Doukhan, *Secrets of Daniel*, 163.

17. Ellen G. White, *Prophets and Kings* (Mountain View, CA: Pacific Press®, 1943), 571.

18. White, *Prophets and Kings*, 572.

19. Bill Gaither and Gloria Gaither, "Because He Lives" (Alexandria, IN: Gaither Music, 1971).

20. Ellen G. White, *The Desire of Ages* (Mountain View, CA: Pacific Press®, 1940), 224, 225.

21. Ellen G. White, *Testimonies for the Church*, vol. 9 (Mountain View, CA: Pacific Press®, 1948), 286.

12

CHAPTER

From North and South to the Beautiful Land

Daniel 11 is probably the longest, most detailed prophecy of the Bible. It mentions wars, persecution, and suffering in connection with alliances and conflicts. National politics, world governments, and power plays involving nations and ideological factions seem overwhelming. All of this can easily cause believers to retreat or, just as dangerously, to embrace worldly methods to advance God's work. Many Christians have fallen into either of these extremes. Some have cowed before the challenge, while others have joined the world in an attempt to advance God's kingdom.

Beyond this important lesson, what else can we can learn from Daniel 11 that is relevant and meaningful to our lives? This complex chapter shows that the powers of the world by themselves can neither thwart nor advance God's work. This truth is of great practical significance. In times of personal uncertainty, whether we face financial, health, or another crisis, we can cling firmly to God, knowing that everything is subject to His sovereignty. Even when evil is perpetrated against us, God can turn it into something good (Genesis 50:20).

Broadly speaking, critical scholarship views Daniel 11 as spanning the war between the Seleucid and Ptolemaic rulers to the reign of Antiochus IV, who presumably stands as the main protagonist of verses 21–45.[1] Conservative evangelical scholars tend to follow this outline until verse 35 but view verses 36–45 as describing the actions of a future antichrist.[2]

Seventh-day Adventists view the major prophetic outlines of Daniel as paralleling one another and spanning history from the prophet's time to the establishment of God's kingdom. Consequently, Daniel 11 most likely recapitulates Daniel 8 and 9, expanding on certain aspects of the previous prophecy.

In this regard, most Seventh-day Adventist students of Daniel agree, although the precise points when pagan Rome and papal Rome respectively arise in the story remain a matter of debate. The main positions can be summarized like this:

> *The Seventh-day Adventist Bible Commentary* and M. Maxwell see the Roman entry in verse 14; R. A. Anderson, G. M. Price, and W. H. Shea believe the Romans come on the scene in verse 16. J. B. Doukhan believes that the Romans appear briefly only in verse 4 and from verse 5 he has the Papacy as the king of the north until the end of the chapter. Maxwell applies verses 21–45 to the Papacy; Shea has the Papacy enter the story in verse 23; Price in verse 30; and *The Seventh-day Adventist Bible Commentary* and Anderson believe that not until verse 31 can we discern the activities of the Papacy.[3]

This study will adopt a position on the issues mentioned above but without any dogmatic pretense. To understand the broad contours of the prophecy and its climax remains more important than pinpointing the major players' entry into the flow of the narrative. However, a comparison with Daniel 8 and 9 offers clues to the flow of events depicted in Daniel 11.

A comparison between Daniel 11 and 8[4]

Daniel 11	Daniel 8, 9
11:2: Persian kingdom	8:3, 20: The Persian ram
11:2 Greek kingdom	8:5, 21: Greek goat
11:3: Mighty Greek king	8:5, 21: Large Greek horn as the first king
11:4: Greek Empire splits into four	8:8, 22: Greek horn broken into four
11:16: Glorious Land conquered	8:9: Glorious Land conquered by pagan Rome
11:22: Prince of the covenant broken	9:26: Messiah cut off by pagan Rome[5]
11:31: "Daily" taken away	8:11: "Daily" taken away by the little horn
11:40: Time of the end	8:17: Time of the end
11:45: King of the north destroyed	8:25: Little horn broken without human hands

Daniel 11 focuses on the kings of the north and the south because God's people, living between the warring parties, would be affected by the war and, ultimately, become the target of the final attack. However, as the prophecy reaches its climax, it becomes evident that the God who stands above and behind the unfolding military, political, and religious events will destroy the enemy.

Persia and Greece

The prophecy opens with a review of Persian history, with a note on the transition to Greece (Daniel 11:2–4): "Behold, three more kings will arise in Persia, and the fourth shall be far richer than them all; by his strength, through his riches, he shall stir up all against the realm of Greece" (verse 2). Since the prophecy is given in the reign of Cyrus (559–530 B.C.) coregent with Darius, the kings may be listed as follows:

1. Cambyses II (530–522 B.C.)
2. False Smerdis (522 B.C.)
3. Darius I Hystaspes (522–486 B.C.)
4. Xerxes I (486–465 B.C.), the Ahasuerus of Esther[6]

According to Herodotus, Xerxes took as many as two million men to attack Athens in 480 B.C. According to the Greek historian, the Persians also attempted to bribe the Greek leaders by distributing gold and riches among them.[7] After an initial success, Xerxes's fleet was eventually defeated at Salamis. As a result, the Persians lost influence in Macedonia and Thrace, which allowed the subsequent rise of Macedonia.[8]

It is helpful to note, however, that several other kings arose from Persia until the Greeks replaced the Persians as the world power.[9] So the mention of three kings, plus one additional Persian king, does not intend to be a thorough account of Persian history. Rather, it only takes the history of Persia to the point of its intersection with Greece, which set in motion a chain of events that led to the rise of the Greco-Macedonian Empire and provided Alexander with a reason to inspire his soldiers to conquer Persia more than a century later.

Alexander the Great rose to the throne of Macedonia in 336 B.C. and in a few years established an empire from Turkey to India. But "when he has arisen, his kingdom shall be broken up and divided toward the four winds of heaven" (verse 4). Alexander died of a fever in 323 B.C. at the age of thirty-three. In the years that followed, Alexander's half-brother Philip and infant, Alexander IV, became nominal rulers for a short time but were soon murdered.[10] Eventually, four of Alexander's generals split the empire among themselves: Cassander took over Macedonia, Lysimachus ruled over Thrace and northwestern Asia Minor, Seleucus I Nicator took possession of Syria and Babylonia, and Ptolemy I Soter became the king of Egypt. The following verses focus on Seleucus and Ptolemy and their respective dynasties that ruled the north and the south of the Holy Land, respectively. Hence, the designations *king of the north* and *king of the south* refer to the rulers of Syria and Egypt, respectively. Such designations, which begin as references to geopolitical entities, eventually acquire symbolic contours.

Hellenistic dynasties of Syria and Egypt

Most students of Daniel view Daniel 11:5–15 as portraying the wars between the Seleucid and Ptolemaic dynasties, although disagreements may arise as to which specific ruler or military event is in view in each verse. The interchange between south and north begins with Ptolemy as king of the south and Seleucus as king of the north. Expelled from Babylon by his rival Antigonus, Seleucus sought protection under Ptolemy, the king of Egypt, and became one of Ptolemy's princes or generals. But subsequently, with the help of Ptolemy, Seleucus regained the lost territories and became stronger than his benefactor (verse 5). Years later, following a costly war, the two kingdoms sealed a peace by the marriage of Antiochus II Theos, the grandson of Seleucus, to Berenice, a daughter of Ptolemy II. However, the agreement did not work out as expected. After Ptolemy II's death, Laodice, the former wife of Antiochus, orchestrated the execution of Antiochus, Berenice, and Berenice's son (verse 6).

Such a turn of events provoked the angry reaction of Ptolemy III, Berenice's brother. He invaded the territory of the northern king, inflicted a great defeat on the enemy, and returned victoriously, carrying booty and the gods of the Syrians to Egypt (verses 7, 8). As the prophecy unfolds and successive kings rise to the throne in both kingdoms, the wars between the north (Syria) and south (Egypt) continue (verses 9–15). The war mentioned in verse 14 likely refers to the Battle of Panium (200 B.C.),[11] when Antiochus III defeated the Ptolemies and the Holy Land passed to Seleucid dominion.

Subsequently, the "violent men of your people shall exalt themselves in fulfillment of the vision, but they shall fall" (verse 14). The "violent men" have been variously understood as a reference to (1) the Syrians under Antiochus IV, who would perpetrate violence against the Jews; (2) the Romans, who eventually would deprive the Jews of their freedom and destroy the temple; and (3) nationalist Jews, who saw the current crisis as an opportunity to further their agenda. That the violent men would rise to fulfill "the vision" seems to point to the Maccabees, whose uprising may have been a human attempt to provide the deliverance of God's people announced in Daniel's vision. Interestingly, Judas Maccabeus (1 Maccabees 8:17–32) and his brothers Jonathan (1 Maccabees 12:1–4, 16) and Simon (1 Maccabees 14:16–24) took the first steps to seek the protection of Rome. Later, John Hyrcanus made a treaty with the Romans so that he would obtain protection. Yet the Roman friendship soon changed into guardianship and eventually led to the full submission of Judea to the Romans.[12]

Finally, the attack of the king of the north against the king of the south (Daniel 11:15) may refer to Antiochus IV's campaign against Egypt in 169/168 B.C. "The focus of that campaign centered around Pelusium, the major city guarding the entrance into the eastern delta of Egypt. Pelusium fell to the troops of Antiochus IV during the campaign, and thus he conquered the eastern half of the delta. Then he returned to Syria for the winter of 169/168 B.C. That was a major error in strategy, and it led to the introduction of the next power in the prophecy."[13]

In summary, Daniel 11:5–15 describes the wars of the Ptolemaic and Seleucid dynasties that consumed the two main divisions of Alexander's empire. The following table summarizes the main actors and the wars they waged:

Wars of the Ptolemaic and Seleucid dynasties, Daniel 11:5-15

Daniel 11	Identification	Syrian Wars[14]
Verse 5	King of the south: Ptolemy I Soter, king of Egypt King of the north: Seleucus I Nicator, king of Syria	
Verses 6–9	Ptolemy II Philadelphus vs. Antiochus I Soter	First Syrian War (274–271 B.C.)
	Antiochus II Theos vs. Ptolemy II Philadelphus	Second Syrian War (260–253 B.C.)
	Ptolemy III Euergetes vs. Seleucus II Callinicus	Third Syrian War (246–241 B.C.)
Verses 10–13	Antiochus III Magnus vs. Ptolemy IV Philopator	Fourth Syrian War (219–217 B.C.)
Verses 14, 15	Antiochus III Magnus vs. Ptolemy V Epiphanes	Fifth Syrian War (202–200 B.C.)
	Antiochus IV Epiphanes vs. Ptolemaic government (under the protection of Rome)	Sixth Syrian War (170–168 B.C.)

Pagan Rome

After the attack of the king of the north (Antiochus IV) against the south, which is reported in verse 15, a new warrior appears in verse 16, not as a king of the north or south but as "he who comes." He also "shall do according to his own will" (verse 16); this expression is used earlier to stress the rise of Greece (verse 3) and used here to introduce a new power. This new ruler or power comes against "him," which most likely refers to the "king of the North" mentioned in verse 15. Although he will wage war against the king of the south, he and his successors are never designated as "king of the North" until verse 45. A major action of this new king concerns the "Glorious Land," where he would stand "with destruction in his power" (verse 16).

From this short description, it appears that pagan Rome is the most likely referent for this new king. After all, Rome came to the rescue of Egypt when it was under attack by the forces of Antiochus IV. After that memorable humiliation by the Roman power, Antiochus IV fades away, and Rome begins to emerge as the dominant power in the ancient Near East. But the strongest argument to identify this new king with Rome lies in the conquest of the "Glorious Land," which, according to the parallel reference in Daniel 8:9, refers to the Roman conquest of the Holy Land.

As the prophecy unfolds, there arises "one who imposes taxes on the glorious kingdom" (Daniel 11:20). Historicist interpreters have identified this ruler as Caesar Augustus, who ordered the census that led to Jesus' birth in Bethlehem (Luke 2:1). Next, the prophecy predicts the rise of "a vile person" who has no legitimate claim to the throne and who destroys the "prince of the covenant" (Daniel 11:21, 22). Of several Roman emperors, Tiberius, the successor of Augustus, seems to fit this prediction. Tiberius was not a natural son of Augustus, but the son of his wife Livia by a priest, also named Tiberius. Augustus reluctantly made him his successor for lack of an alternative. It has been pointed out that "Tiberius could act with consummate hypocrisy, bore grudges and could be cruel to his enemies, was always suspicious, hated to be forced to make his meaning clear and was never eager to come to an irrevocable decision."[15] Although the previous characteristics could be said of some other rulers, the fact that he destroyed the "prince of the covenant" (verse 22) makes his identification with the prophecy virtually certain, since, according to Daniel 9:26, the Messiah was to be cut off by pagan Rome.

Some students of Daniel view Daniel 11:23 as introducing papal Rome,[16] while others contend that the following verses continue with Imperial Rome.[17] Indeed, it appears that Daniel 11:23–28, like Daniel 8, goes back in history. After depicting how Rome "grew exceedingly great," Daniel 8 describes the rise of Rome (verses 9, 23–25).

Such a depiction matches the rise of pagan Rome. As history shows, Rome grew from a city-state into a world empire. It entered into a "league of friendship"[18] with the Jews to protect them, but subsequently, it acted deceitfully and imposed its dominion on them, eventually destroying their temple (A.D. 70). Interestingly, a common institution in ancient Rome was the *foedus* (ritual alliance), which "could define all relationships Romans might experience, whether political, civil, international, amicable, amorous, or cosmological."[19] Thus, by means of such *foedera* (alliances), the Romans would seal diplomatic relationships with different nations and establish their rulership over those they vowed to protect.

Papal Rome

A transition of some sort seems to be indicated in Daniel 11:29. As the Roman power undertakes another attack against the south, this time "it shall not be like the former or the latter" (verse 29). This expression appears to introduce a change of circumstances. Regardless of how the expression is interpreted, the subsequent verses depict an entity whose actions are predominantly religious in nature (verses 30–39). He will give attention to those who have abandoned the "holy covenant"; he will "defile the sanctuary," "take away the daily," "magnify himself above every god," and "speak blasphemies against" God (verses 30, 31, 36). In addition, he fiercely persecutes those "of understanding," and many "fall by sword and flame, by captivity and plundering" (verses 33, 35).

The description of the emerging power and its hostility toward God's people reverberates the description of the little horn in Daniel 7 and 8. In addition, the desecration of the sanctuary and the self-exaltation undertaken by this power point to the prophetic depictions of the kings of Babylon and Tyre (Isaiah 14:12–14; Ezekiel 28:12–19). In fact, a number of actions and teachings carried out by the papacy are consistent with the portrayal of the power that enters the scene of action after Daniel 11:29. Clearly, the sacrament of the Mass, auricular confession, penance, purgatory, and indulgences function as a counterfeit plan of salvation, distorting and competing with Christ's intercessory ministry in the heavenly sanctuary.

A few comments on the major aspects of the papacy's work, as depicted in this section of Daniel, may be helpful. First, this power desecrates the sanctuary, which, according to the parallel between Daniel 8:11 and 11:31, points to the heavenly sanctuary. Such desecration happens at the spiritual-theological level. For example, when the earthly power claims to offer forgiveness on the basis of human works—penance and almsgiving—it obscures the message of justification by faith and obliterates the ministry of Christ in the heavenly temple. Furthermore, in doing so, it casts down the foundation of the sanctuary, which rests on righteousness and mercy (Psalm 97:2).

Second, by joining itself to the state, a process facilitated by Constantine and eventually implemented by subsequent emperors, the papacy brings about the abomination of desolation and becomes a persecuting power. Such an abomination "may be described as a union of the secular and the religious—the state and the church—in which the religious aspect is defiled by its merging with the functions of the state."[20] By wielding state power, the Roman Church carried out the Crusades, which increased the power and intolerance of the papacy toward its opponents.

Also, it is helpful to mention that the Inquisition became one of the institutions established by Rome to enforce spiritual unity by a temporal authority.[21] The seeds of such a system may have already been found in Augustine, who endorsed "the theory that the State has a right to interfere in constraining men to keep within the Church. Starting with a forced interpretation of the words, '*Compel* them to come in,' in Luke xiv.23, he [Augustine] enunciates principles of coercion which, though in him they were subdued and rendered practically of little moment by the spirit of love which formed so large an element in his character, yet found their natural development in the despotic intolerance of the Papacy, and the horrors of the Inquisition."[22]

Third, the self-exaltation of the papacy manifests itself in the titles borne by the pope and his claim to infallibility. "In addition to the Bishop of Rome, which is his primary title, the pope has several other titles: Vicar of Peter, Vicar of Jesus Christ, Successor of the Chief of the Apostles, Supreme Pontiff of the Universal Church, Primate of Italy, Archbishop and

Metropolitan of the Roman Province, Sovereign of Vatican City State, and Servant of the Servants of God."[23] The doctrine of infallibility, ascribed to the bishop of Rome and to the body of bishops, further emphasizes the pretensions of the papacy.[24] This goes hand in hand with the pope's self-appointed authority, according to which he "enjoys, by divine institution, 'supreme, full, immediate, and universal power in the care of souls.' "[25]

Final events

The vision of Daniel 11:40–45 outlines major events leading to the close of human history. But before any interpretation can be suggested, we must pay close attention to the context and imagery portrayed in the passage to understand clearly what the text says. At the outset, it should be noted that the title *king of the north* occurred for the last time in verse 15 in reference to a Seleucid king. Although the pagan Roman Empire (verses 16–28) and papal Rome (verses 29–39) are not designated as the "king of the North," they act as such. These two successive powers at times engage the "king of the South," seeming to indicate that they represent two additional phases of the king of the north. The "king of the North" referred to in verse 40 seems to be a continuation or another phase of the previous power, which makes an ominous appearance at the time of the end.

As we proceed, two interrelated background concepts must be observed. First, the king of the north appears as a warrior leading a military expedition. Significantly, Yahweh often appears in the Old Testament as a warrior. Even the tabernacle in the middle of the Israelite camp can be conceived as the tent of the Divine Warrior, surrounded by His military units.[26] A dim reflection of this image emerges as the king of the north sets the "tents of his palace" between the seas and Mount Zion (verse 45). Therefore, the king of the north in his military enterprise performs actions that are predicated on Yahweh, the Divine Warrior.[27] In other words, the king sets himself against Yahweh and aims at taking Yahweh's rightful position as the Divine Warrior. Second, allusions to the Exodus reverberate throughout the passage, as shown by a groundbreaking study on this subject.[28] In this study, both the king of the north and God go to Egypt. While God goes there to free His people, the king marches to the south to conquer Egypt. The mention of "chariots" and "horsemen" also relates to the Exodus from Egypt (verse 40). Interestingly, Edom, Moab, and Ammon were not conquered by the Israelites nor by the king of the north. Moreover, like the Israelites, the king of the north also carried silver and gold from Egypt. While the Israelites left the land of Egypt to meet the Lord on Mount Sinai, the king leaves Egypt to attack Mount Zion.

As we consider the Divine Warrior and the Exodus motifs reflected in the passage, it appears that the king of the north

> is pretending to act like God by defeating Egypt, by claiming to have control over history, and by determining who should live and who should die. He goes down to Egypt with his army, then leaves to Canaan, and finally places his tent in the center of his military camp in preparation for a war of extermination. The king also pretends to be like the people of God: he goes down to Egypt, possesses the wealth of Egypt, leaves Egypt, and is involved in a war of extermination. But he is in fact the enemy of God's people.[29]

Verses 40–45 portray a collage of military images found elsewhere in the Old Testament. It all begins when the king of the south attacks the king of the north in the time of the end (verse 40). This event refers to the pope's capture by General Berthier in 1798, in the context of a secular attack against religion, set in motion by the French Revolution. This event fulfills the prophetic word about the mortal wound inflicted on the first beast of Revelation 13. Note that in the symbolism of Daniel 11, the king of the south stands for Egypt and represents secularism and atheism. In Exodus 5:2, Pharaoh says: "Who is the LORD, that I should obey His voice to let Israel go? I do not know the LORD, nor will I let Israel go." Ellen G.

White, commenting on this episode in the context of Revelation 11, concurs that Egypt represents atheism and applies the symbolism to France in the context of the French Revolution.[30]

In response to the attack of the south, the king of the north mounts an invasion that overwhelms the enemy. This indicates that the mortal wound is healed. So the papacy begins to reinforce its ranks to face the challenges of atheism and secularism and recover its prestige as a world religious power. Today, "Egypt represents the nations of the earth that do not take the Lord into consideration. Today we would probably refer to them as non-Christian societies and nations where secularism or atheism prevails. In the final conflict these nations will join the king of the North in his opposition against the Lord. This understanding of Egypt fits well with Daniel 11, where the main interest of the chapter is the cosmic conflict and the forces involved in it. Behind military and political powers are operating specific ideologies."[31]

In describing the northern counterattack as a flood and whirlwind (Daniel 11:40), the passage evokes prophetic descriptions of God bringing judgment against sinners: "Like a tempest of hail and a destroying storm, like a flood of mighty waters overflowing, who will bring them down to the earth with His hand" (Isaiah 28:2). Similar imagery also occurs in reference to the Assyrians invading Judah: "He will pass through Judah, He will overflow and pass over, He will reach up to the neck" (Isaiah 8:8).

The imagery here is that of an invading army: the king of the north storms against the south as a flood and a whirlwind. But on his way to the south, he passes through the Glorious Land (Daniel 11:41), as did the Assyrian and Babylonian armies on their way to Egypt. As they pass through the Holy Land, they leave behind a trail of devastation. Likewise, the king of the north passes through the Holy Land, "and tens of thousands shall fall" (verse 41, ESV). This may refer to the attack launched by the forces of evil against God's people by means of miracles to deceive the dwellers of the earth (Revelation 13:13,

14). It will be a time of refinement before the final crisis (Revelation 3:14–22).[32] Ellen G. White writes, "Wonderful scenes, with which Satan will be closely connected, will soon take place. God's Word declares that Satan will work miracles. He will make people sick, and then will suddenly remove from them his satanic power. They will then be regarded as healed. These works of apparent healing will bring Seventh-day Adventists to the test. Many who have had great light will fail to walk in the light, because they have not become one with Christ."[33]

Nevertheless, some will escape: Edom, Moab, and Ammon lay in Transjordan and did not stand in the way of the northern military expedition (Daniel 11:41). Incidentally, with regards to these nations, the Old Testament not only announces judgment on them but also includes their restoration and incorporation into God's people in Messianic times (Jeremiah 49:6; Amos 9:12; Isaiah 11:14). In the context of the cosmic conflict, these nations may represent people from all Christian communities and world religions who will come out of Babylon and join the eschatological remnant (Revelation 12:17).[34]

But at this point, the king of the north's main goal is to conquer Egypt. Eventually, he succeeds and takes possession of "the treasures of gold and silver, and . . . all the precious things of Egypt" (Daniel 11:43). However, the king of the north not only conquered Egypt but also made the Libyans and Ethiopians submit to him (verse 43). Note that these two countries sat at the western and southern borders of Egypt, respectively. The king going beyond the borders of Egypt points to the success of the campaign. At this juncture, the king of the north becomes incredibly rich and powerful, ruling over a confederation of nations, reminding us of the gathering of the nations for the eschatological battle (Ezekiel 38:5–7).[35] Significantly, as the prophecy unfolds the symbolism of the king of the north, which at first represents the papacy, it becomes an embodiment of the mystical Babylon depicted in the book of Revelation.

The king of the north seems unstoppable, but at the height of his military success, "news from the east and the north" greatly disturbs him (Daniel 11:44). If the king was in Ethiopia at the time, the news might have come from the Holy Land.[36] The text does not relay the content of the bad news, but a king on a campaign could risk a rebellion elsewhere in his realm, or a rival king may have appeared to claim the throne. This image reminds one of Sennacherib, who, after hearing a rumor, returned to his land and was killed (Isaiah 37:7; 2 Kings 19:7). Angered by the bad news, the king now reverses the direction of his expedition.

The news from "the east and the north" may refer to the events described in Revelation 18:1, 2, which portrays an angel proclaiming a powerful message against Babylon, reiterating the three angels' message (Revelation 14:6–12), announcing the fall of Babylon. This message comes when Babylon has the support of the kings of the earth (Revelation 17:11–13) and has much gold and silver (Revelation 18:12, 16). Such news horrifies and enrages the king of the north.[37]

Then he marches from the south to the north (from Egypt to Mount Zion), leading a confederation of nations to "destroy and annihilate many" (Daniel 11:44). The verb *annihilate* comes from the vocabulary of a holy war in connection with God's instructions to destroy the Canaanites and other enemies. Eventually, the king of the north sets his military camp between the seas and the "glorious holy mountain" (verse 45), that is, between the Mediterranean Sea and the Dead Sea, which frame the Holy Land, with Mount Zion in between. Revelation 16:16 designates the same potential battlefield as Armageddon.

At this point, the prophecy of Daniel 11:40–45 depicts the final attack of the forces of evil, with the intention of exterminating God's people (Revelation 13:15–17).[38] According to Ellen G. White, the "great deceiver" says:

> When once we have the power, we will show what we can do with those who will not swerve from their allegiance to God. We led the Romish church to inflict imprisonment, torture, and death upon those who refused to yield to her decrees; and now that we are bringing the Protestant churches and the world into

> harmony with this right arm of our strength, we will finally have a law to exterminate all who will not submit to our authority. When death shall be made the penalty of violating our sabbath, then many who are now ranked with commandment keepers will come over to our side.[39]

But as the king of the north stands poised to attack Jerusalem, "he shall come to his end, and no one will help him" (Daniel 11:45). The final phrase "no one will help him" points to the irreversible end of the king of the north, implying a supernatural intervention. In other words, the Lord personally intervenes, delivers His people, and defeats the evil forces. As Scripture says, "The Lamb will overcome them, for He is Lord of lords and King of kings" (Revelation 17:14).

Conclusion

In the third year of Cyrus, a "great conflict" raged between the spiritual forces attempting to influence earthly events related to God's people (Daniel 10:1). In Daniel 11, this great conflict spiraled into a war between east and west (Persia and Greece), followed by wars between the king of the north and the king of the south. God's people are caught in between the warring factions and suffer persecution. As the battle unfolds, the protagonists change. At first, the Seleucids fight against the Ptolemies (verses 5–15); next, pagan Rome arises and overshadows the former powers (verses 16–28); then, papal Rome grows out of pagan Rome (verses 29–39); and finally, papal Rome reemerges in the time of the end as the king of the north.

In the time of the end, after the capture of the pope by the secular forces of France, the papacy begins to recover its prestige and authority, eventually waging war against its secular opponents and the people of God. Although it will succeed in gathering a coalition of nations to launch a final attack against God's people, it will fail because God will intervene. God's people will be delivered, and the evil coalition will be obliterated.

At this point, one may ask, How plausible is this scenario?

Is there any probability that the institution of the papacy will eventually embody the character of the king of the north? Or is this just alarmist speculation fueled by anti-Catholic prejudice?

An evangelical scholar offers this answer:

> Luther, Calvin, the seventeenth-century Protestant confessions, the Puritans, Wesley, Spurgeon, et al., believed that the papacy (not this or that Pope) is the institution out of which the Anti-Christ will eventually come. I share this broad protestant consensus. The papacy claims christological and pneumatological titles and prerogatives (e.g. vicar of Christ, infallible teacher, supreme head of the church with full, immediate and universal power), coupling them with earthly political power. Remember that Popes are monarchs of a sovereign political state. In the papacy what belongs to God and what belongs to Caesar tragically intermingle. This poisoned mixture is the potential milieu for the Anti-Christ to rise from.[40]

---

1. See, e.g., James A. Montgomery, *A Critical and Exegetical Commentary on the Book of Daniel*, International Critical Commentary (New York: Charles Scribner's Sons, 1927), 418–468.

2. Andrew E. Steinmann, *Daniel*, Concordia Commentary (Saint Louis, MO: Concordia Pub., 2008), 495–555.

3. Gerhard Pfandl, *Daniel: The Seer of Babylon* (Hagerstown, MD: Review and Herald®, 2004), 106. For a detailed study, see Hotma Saor Parasian Silitonga, "Continuity and Change in World Rulers: A Comparative Study and Evaluation of Seventh-day Adventist Interpretations of Daniel 11" (PhD diss., Adventist International Institute of Advanced Studies, 2001).

4. Adapted from William H. Shea, *Daniel 7–12*, Abundant Life Bible Amplifier (Nampa, ID: Pacific Press®, 1996), 179. See also Pfandl, *Daniel*, 106–108.

5. Daniel 9 explains the vision of Daniel 8.

6. Shea, *Daniel 7–12*, 179, 180.

7. Pierre Briant, *From Cyrus to Alexander: A History of the Persian Empire* (Winona Lake, IN: Eisenbrauns, 2002), 532.

8. Michael Axworthy, *Empire of the Mind: A History of Iran* (London: C. Hurst, 2007), 25.

9. Artaxerxes I Longimanus (465–424 B.C.); Darius II (423–405 B.C.); Artaxerxes II Mnemon (404–359 B.C.); Artaxerxes III Ochus (358–338 B.C.); Arses (337–336 B.C.); Darius III Codomannus (336–330 B.C.).

10. Robin Lane Fox, *Classical World: The Epic History of Greece and Rome* (London: Penguin, 2006), 241–251.

11. John D. Grainger, *The Syrian Wars*, Mnemosyne Supplements, vol. 320 (Leiden: Brill, 2010), 257.

12. Siegfried H. Horn, *The Seventh-day Adventist Bible Dictionary* (Washington, DC: Review and Herald®, 1979), 951.

13. Shea, *Daniel 7–12*, 187.

14. F. W. Walbank, A. E. Astin, M. W. Frederiksen, R. M. Ogilvie, eds., *The Hellenistic World*, 2nd ed., Cambridge Ancient History, vol. 7, pt. 1 (Cambridge: Cambridge University Press, 1984); Grainger, *The Syrian Wars*.

15. Robin Seager, *Tiberius*, 2nd ed. (Malden, MA: Blackwell, 2005), 236.

16. See, e.g., Shea, *Daniel 7–12*, 195–197.

17. See, e.g., Uriah Smith, *Thoughts, Critical and Practical, on the Book of Daniel*, 2nd ed. (Battle Creek, MI: Seventh-day Adventist Pub. Assn., 1881), 318–320.

18. The underlying Hebrew expression is a plural verbal form *hitḥabbrût* (literally, "they joined one another") that carries the meaning of "to make an alliance" or "have partnership with." Francis Brown, Samuel Rolles Driver, and Charles Augustus Briggs, *Enhanced Brown-Driver-Briggs Hebrew and English Lexicon* (Oxford: Clarendon Press, 1977), 288.

19. Bill Gladhill, *Rethinking Roman Alliance: A Study in Poetics and Society* (Cambridge: Cambridge University Press, 2016), 2.

20. Shea, *Daniel 7–12*, 204, 205.

21. J. R. King, preface to "On Baptism, Against the Donatists," in *St. Augustine: The Writings Against the Manichaeans and Against the Donatists*, vol. 4, Nicene and Post-Nicene Fathers 1 (Buffalo, NY: Christian Literature, 1887), 406.

22. King, preface, 406; emphasis in the original.

23. Richard P. McBrien, *The Church: The Evolution of Catholicism* (London: HarperCollins, 2008), 93.

24. United States Conference of Catholic Bishops, *Catechism of the Catholic Church*, 2nd ed. (Washington, DC: United States Catholic Conference, 2000), 235, 236.

25. Conference of Catholic Bishops, *Catechism of the Catholic Church*, 246.

26. Michael M. Homan, "The Divine Warrior in His Tent: A Military Model for Yahweh's Tabernacle," *Bible Review* 16, no. 6 (December 2000): 22–33, 55.

27. For an overview of the Divine Warrior motif in the Bible, see Tremper Longman III and Daniel G. Reid, *God Is a Warrior*, Studies in Old Testament Biblical Theology (Grand Rapids, MI: Zondervan, 1995).

28. Ángel Manuel Rodríguez, "Daniel 11 and the Islam Interpretation," *Biblical Research Institute Release* 13, May 2015, 9.

29. Rodriguez, "Daniel 11," 10.

30. Ellen G. White, *The Great Controversy* (Mountain View, CA: Pacific Press®, 1950), 269.

31. Rodríguez, "Daniel 11," 17.

32. Rodríguez, "Daniel 11," 23–25.

33. Ellen G. White, *Selected Messages*, book 2 (Washington, DC: Review and Herald®, 1958), 53.

34. Rodríguez, "Daniel 11," 20.

35. Carol A. Newsom, *Daniel: A Commentary*, Old Testament Library (Louisville, KY: Westminster John Knox Press, 2014), 358.

36. Jacques B. Doukhan, *Secrets of Daniel: Wisdom and Dreams of a Jewish Prince in Exile* (Hagerstown, MD: Review and Herald®, 2000), 176.

37. Rodríguez, "Daniel 11," 22, 23.

38. Rodríguez, "Daniel 11," 25, 26.

39. Ellen G. White, *Testimonies to Ministers and Gospel Workers* (Mountain View, CA: Pacific Press®, 1944), 473.

40. Leonardo de Chirico, "Ten Questions With Leonardo de Chirico," *Credo Magazine* 5, no. 4 (November 2015): 10.

CHAPTER 13

From Dust to Stars

Daniel 1 reports Nebuchadnezzar taking captives to Babylon, but Daniel 12 portrays Michael standing up to deliver God's people from spiritual Babylon. In each of the narratives and prophecies of Daniel, the end arrives with the defeat of God's enemies. Whether it is Belshazzar, the conspirators in Darius's court, the little horn, or the king of the north, they all get destroyed. Daniel 12 reaffirms this truth and introduces something new: death itself will be obliterated. But until that grand and glorious day dawns, there will be a time of waiting, of trouble, and of brutal persecution. Just when the evil powers appear to prevail, Michael will stand up to vindicate His people and deal a crushing blow to the enemy.

As we study Daniel 12, it is helpful to remember that this chapter belongs to the final vision, consisting of a prologue (Daniel 10), the vision proper (Daniel 11:1–12:4), and an epilogue (Daniel 12:5–13). Daniel 12 not only concludes the last vision but also closes the entire book while exploring three main themes: the rise of Michael, the hope of resurrection, and the time of waiting that is announced in the vision.

The rise of Michael

Although mentioned for the first time by name in Daniel

10:13, Michael emerges as the most important character in the book of Daniel. He appeared as the fourth Man in the blazing furnace (Daniel 3), the "Son of Man" in the heavenly judgment (Daniel 7), the "Prince of the host" in the heavenly sanctuary (Daniel 8), the "Messiah" who was cut off in the middle of the seventieth week (Daniel 9), and the "man clothed in linen" above the river (Daniel 10). In Daniel 10, we noted that Michael serves as the Commander of God's army, usually appears in warfare contexts, and His name means "who is like God!"[1] Indeed, Michael is none other than the preincarnate Son of God (Jude 9; Revelation 12:7; see the discussion on Daniel 10). Further reflection on this glorious figure reveals three characteristics of Michael.

First, He "shall stand up" (*'āmad*) (Daniel 12:1). In military contexts, the verb means "to take a position" or "form up."[2] Thus, the term belongs to the vocabulary of warfare[3] and occurs a number of times in Daniel 11. Several rulers "stand up," one after another, to wage war against a competitor and become the new king in the respective historical, geopolitical, or religious contexts depicted in the prophecy (Daniel 11:2, 3, 4, 7, 8, 14, 16, 20; see also Daniel 8:3, 6, 22, 23, 25).[4]

Michael stands up as the final and definitive King, who overcomes the previous power (Daniel 11:45), and establishes Himself as the King of the new cosmic order. Michael's final victory at the end outshines Nebuchadnezzar's fleeting victory at the beginning. Jerusalem eclipses Babylon. The city that lost in the beginning becomes the victor, and in the end, the city that previously won disappears forever. And now, "the ruler from heaven will take over, and He will make up a very different type of kingdom, one that is ruled upon the principles of righteousness."[5]

Second, He is the "great prince" (*śar*) (verse 1). Among other uses, the word *prince* may designate a ruler or "the highest commander in a military (1 Chronicles 11:6)."[6] In the vision shown to Joshua shortly before the conquest of Jericho, the heavenly being who appeared—most likely the preincarnate Christ—introduced Himself as "commander [*śar*] of the LORD's army" (Joshua 5:15). Also, a synonym of this word (*nāgîd*) is applied to the Messiah (Daniel 9:25). In addition to the military connotation, it should be noted that the term *prince* also occurs as a "technical term for the high priest of Israel; see 1 Chron. 15:22; Ezra 8:24; Dan. 10:5."[7] This fact will be relevant for the discussion of the third point below.

Thus, the designation of Michael as "prince" certainly carries military and royal connotations, as conveyed by the combination with the verb "stand up" (*'āmad*), which certainly echoes the various military uses of this verb in Daniel 11. Insofar as the term *prince* relates to the phrase "Michael shall stand up," the "prince" emerges as a military commander who will take over the rulership once held by the kings of the world.

Third, He is the one "who stands" (*'ōmēd*) for God's people (Daniel 12:1). The verb "to stand" appears here in a slightly different grammatical construction than above. The idea is that Michael stands *for* God's people, as conveyed by the King James Version. Some versions translate the phrase with the sense that the prince watches over or protects (e.g., NAB, NET, NIV, NRSV). Although these translations are not necessarily wrong, they do not capture the most important connotation of the word in the context of Daniel's message.

In fact, the verb "to stand" also carries a judicial meaning. In the context of court proceedings, the priests "shall stand as judges" (Ezekiel 44:24). Likewise, Yahweh "stands" to judge His people (Isaiah 3:13). But since judges normally sit, a judge would probably stand up to pronounce the verdict (Exodus 18:13; Isaiah 16:5). It seems that as the judgment unfolds, the parties "stand" before the judge, and whoever speaks must also stand (Exodus 18:13; Numbers 35:12).[8] Thus, our passage depicts Michael standing in the heavenly tribunal to defend the cause of His people;[9] this idea is corroborated by the mention of "the book"[10] (Daniel 12:1; cf. Daniel 7:18, 22, 27), which contains the names of those that are delivered by Michael.

It is important to keep in mind that this revelation about Michael as the prince of God's people occurs in the context of unspeakable suffering and anguish. As human history draws to a close, there will be "a time of trouble" like never before (Daniel

12:1). It will take place when the proclamation of the three angels' messages closes, and mercy will no longer be available to impenitent sinners. Christ's intercessory ministry in the heavenly sanctuary will have ceased. Ellen G. White describes the moment:

> When He leaves the sanctuary, darkness covers the inhabitants of the earth. In that fearful time the righteous must live in the sight of a holy God without an intercessor. The restraint which has been upon the wicked is removed, and Satan has entire control of the finally impenitent. God's long-suffering has ended. The world has rejected His mercy, despised His love, and trampled upon His law. The wicked have passed the boundary of their probation; the Spirit of God, persistently resisted, has been at last withdrawn. Unsheltered by divine grace, they have no protection from the wicked one. Satan will then plunge the inhabitants of the earth into one great, final trouble. As the angels of God cease to hold in check the fierce winds of human passion, all the elements of strife will be let loose. The whole world will be involved in ruin more terrible than that which came upon Jerusalem of old.[11]

Despite the ominous events that take place in the time of trouble, we can look to the future with hope and confidence. Jesus, our High Priest, stands for us in the heavenly sanctuary. Because we have accepted Him as Savior and Lord, our names are written in the book of life with His blood. We shall stand protected during the last days of Earth's history. As dark clouds cover the earth, we will walk in the light of Calvary. When human hopes and resources are exhausted, the sea will part, and we walk into heavenly Zion. There we will enjoy the presence of the King forever.

The hope of resurrection

As the book of Daniel unfolds, the picture emerges of God at work to reverse the power of death. By delivering the three

Hebrews from fire and Daniel from the lions, God asserted His authority over death. "The stories in the first half of the book demonstrate without a doubt that God delivers from the *threat* of death, and they prepare for the prophecy in the final vision that predicts deliverance from the *fact* of death."[12]

In this prediction, Daniel makes the most explicit Old Testament statement about the resurrection of the dead: "And many of those who sleep in the dust of the earth shall awake, some to everlasting life, some to shame and everlasting contempt" (verse 2). This concise statement affirms the notion of resurrection already implied in other biblical passages (Job 19:25–27; Isaiah 25; 26:19; 66:24; Psalms 69; 73:24). Here, for the first time, the Bible mentions the idea of a double resurrection. While some will rise to vindication, others will rise to condemnation.

Daniel 12:2 refers to the special resurrection that takes place just before Jesus comes. It involves those who "have been eminent on both sides of the great conflict between good and evil."[13] Two groups are in view: those "who have died in the faith of the third angel's message"[14] (Matthew 26:64; Revelation 14:13), and those who crucified Jesus (Revelation 1:7).[15] While the general resurrection of the righteous occurs at the second coming of Jesus, the resurrection of the wicked occurs at the end of the millennium (Revelation 20:5–10). Furthermore, Daniel 12:2 can be applied to the hope of resurrection in a general sense as well. By raising the righteous from the grave, God reverses the ultimate consequence of sin. As indicated by the connection between Daniel 12:2 and Genesis 3, the resurrection overturns the curse of death that came upon the human race as a consequence of the Fall.

When our first parents violated the command of God, He pronounced the curse:

> By the sweat of your brow will you win your bread
> until you return to the *earth*;
> for from it you were taken.
> Dust you are, to *dust* you will return (Genesis 3:19, REB; emphasis added).

It seems obvious that the passage in Daniel alludes to the narrative of the Fall because of the shared words *death*, *dust*, and *earth*. However, there is another detail that makes this correlation even more explicit. The statement in Daniel literally says: "Those who sleep in the *earth* of *dust* shall awake" (Daniel 12:2; author's translation). Significantly, only in Daniel 12:2 and Genesis 3:19 do the words *earth* and *dust* occur in this sequence, which further indicates the connection between the resurrection and the Fall. Whereas in the Fall, humans return to dust, in the resurrection, they awake from the dust. In other words, in the resurrection, God will reverse the curse by displaying His creative power.

Daniel 12:2 goes on to say that some will awake "to everlasting life" (*ḥayyî 'ôlām*). After the Fall, God expelled Adam (both male and female) from the Garden "lest he put out his hand and take also of the tree of life, and eat, and live forever [*ḥay 'ôlām*]" (Genesis 3:22). Whereas in the Garden, eternal life was forfeited, in the resurrection, eternal life is regained. In the end, God reverses the Fall by overcoming death and restoring the fullness of life (Deuteronomy 30:15–20; Proverbs 8:32–36; Romans 8:35–39). Therefore, those who rise to eternal life "shall shine like the brightness of the firmament, . . . like the stars forever and ever" (Daniel 12:3). What a wonderful restoration—"from dust to stars."[16]

The final verse of the book conveys the resurrection promise to Daniel himself: "And you shall rest and shall stand [*'āmad*] in your allotted place at the end of the days" (verse 13, ESV). "Allotted place," or "inheritance," alludes to the portions allocated to the Israelite tribes in the Promised Land (Joshua 14–18). Just as Michael stands up at the beginning of the chapter, Daniel will stand up at the end; after all, the destiny of Michael and His people are interconnected. Whereas the book begins with Daniel as a captive in Babylon, it concludes with the prophet rising to eternal life—from exile to resurrection. What a reversal!

We may now suffer as the great controversy rages, but a glorious day is fast approaching. Daniel provides a glimpse of this coming glory and the time when God will set all things right and vanquish the last enemy.

The prophetic times

The time of the end comes with unprecedented challenges and opportunities for God's people. It is the period following the 1,260 years of papal supremacy and persecution (Daniel 12:1, 7), extending to the second coming of Jesus. As the time of the end begins, the book of Daniel is unsealed, gathering renewed interest and increased knowledge of its prophetic message (verse 4). As one historian notes: " 'The prophetic days of Daniel had been understood as calendar years by only seven writers in the sixteenth century, and by only twelve in the seventeenth, but they were correctly understood by 21 of the 22 who wrote in the eighteenth, and by over 100 of the 109 who wrote on Daniel between 1800 and 1850.' "[17]

Three specific time periods are mentioned in Daniel 12. The first one occurs in the context of a question asked of "the man clothed in linen," who stood "above the waters of the river": "How long shall the fulfillment of these wonders be?" (verse 6). It is helpful to understand that the term *wonders* (*pĕlā'ôt*) stands for the "blasphemies" (*niplā'ôt*) spoken by the king of the north (papal Rome) in Daniel 11:36. The same word also occurs in Daniel 8:24 to qualify the action of the little horn (papal Rome), which will destroy "fearfully" (*niplā'ôt*). Note also that the "man clothed in linen" (Michael) must be identified with the heavenly figure described earlier in the vision (Daniel 10:4–6).

Although the location remains the same, the river is not referred to as the Tigris (*Hiddekel*) or by the common Hebrew word for river (*nahar*), as in Daniel 10:4. Instead, a different term for *river* (*yĕ'ōr*) occurs here, elsewhere designated as the Nile River (Genesis 41:1; Exodus 1:22). It is from above the waters of the Nile that the man in linen announces: "A time, times, and half a time" (Daniel 12:7)—this is the 1,260 years of papal persecution that were already mentioned in Daniel 7:25. The uncommon term *river* (Nile) is clearly associated with Egypt, the oppression under Pharaoh, and the Exodus. This allusive term likens the papal persecution to the oppression of God's people under Pharaoh. No wonder the Lord stands above the Nile as if ready to strike it and set in motion a new Exodus to free the persecuted church from papal oppression. In swearing "by Him who lives forever" (Daniel 12:7), the man in linen evokes the covenant oath, redeeming His people from the house of bondage (Genesis 15:17, 18; Exodus 2:24; 20:2).

The second prophetic period, extending for "one thousand two hundred and ninety days," begins with the removal of the "daily" and the setting up of "the abomination of desolation" (Daniel 12:11). We already understand from previous prophecies that the "daily" represents Christ's intercessory ministry, obfuscated by the papal system and replaced by a counterfeit plan of salvation—"the abomination of desolation" (Daniel 8:11; 11:31). Since papal domination came to an end in A.D. 1798 when the French forces imprisoned Pope Pius VI, we subtract 1,290 from 1,798 and arrive at A.D. 508. So the question arises, What happened in that year?

It has been argued that the conversion of Clovis, the king of the Franks, to the Catholic faith and his victory over the Goths led to the supremacy of the Catholic Church in the West.[18] Although the date of these events has been a matter of debate, their historical significance is beyond dispute. In regard to Clovis's conversion, one source says: "The conversion of Clovis to Catholicism is an epoch-making event in the history of the world. Its consequences go beyond the limits of the little Frankish kingdom on which the son of Childeric reigned at the end of the fifth century and reverberate through the centuries reaching us."[19]

Some scholars date Clovis's conversion to a few years earlier (A.D. 496), but they recognize that an important event happened in A.D. 508.[20] As one historian remarks, "After defeating the Visigoths in 507, Clovis seized their treasury and gave it to the shrine of St. Martin of Tours. At Tours in 508 Clovis received a cloak from the eastern emperor, completing an alliance in faith with Rome and in politics with Constantinople."[21]

Others view the conversion or baptism as taking place in 508.[22] An in-depth academic study on this subject argues persuasively for a "gradual process of conversion to Catholicism over a number of years which finally culminated in Clovis's baptism and complete commitment to the Catholic faith in 508."[23]

Overall, even if uncertainties remain about the events of A.D. 508, one thing remains clear: "The partnership of throne and altar, the 'abomination that makes desolate,' began. Clovis fought for the church, and the church served Clovis. Between A.D. 508 and 538, decisive blows against the opposition of papal supremacy were achieved, and the political powers symbolized by the three horns were uprooted, allowing the little horn to grow and flourish. The three horns uprooted were the Visigoths, the Vandals, and the Ostrogoths."[24]

The third prophetic period comes with a blessing for the one "who waits, and comes to the one thousand three hundred and thirty-five days" (Daniel 12:12). The context indicates that both the 1,290- and the 1,335-year prophecies began in A.D. 508. Thus, adding 1,335 years to 508 results in 1843. Interestingly, the announcement of this prophetic period does not evoke activity from the little horn (like the 1,260 and the 1,290 years) but only mentions that those living in that time period would be blessed. What kind of blessing would that be? In 1843, the proclamation of the first angel's message was in full course—the judgment was about to begin in heaven. Here we find the blessing for those living in that prophetic time. Those who follow the Lord during the time of that judgment will take part in the special resurrection that precedes the second coming of Jesus (Daniel 12:12; Revelation 14:13).[25]

Finally, the last time reference in the book occurs in the closing verse. Daniel would rest, but the angel assures him that he will arise at the "end of the days" (Daniel 12:13). This phrase closes the book and points to the consummation of all things. It points to the time when "the Lord Himself will descend from heaven with a shout, with the voice of an archangel [Michael!], and with the trumpet of God. And the dead in Christ will rise first" (1 Thessalonians 4:16). We will be part of a kingdom that will stand forever with no transfer to other hands. This glorious vision should be a tremendous encouragement in the midst of our trials and sufferings. Even if we must rest before the breaking of that glorious day, we have the assurance that we will arise with Daniel and the saints of all the ages to receive our inheritance in Christ.

Conclusion

The book of Daniel concludes with the rise of Michael, the promise of resurrection, and significant references to time. Daniel 12 mentions the time of the end and the prophetic periods of 1,260, 1,290, 1,335 years, and it closes with the "end of the days." Such references to prophetic time indicate that God is the Grand Sovereign over the cosmos and our planet. Yet the resurrection promise also reveals that He cares for and guides our personal histories, with all of their challenges, struggles, and victories. With the psalmist, we can confidently say, "My times are in Your hand" (Psalm 31:15). As the journey in this broken world continues, the worst of times may seem overwhelming, but we can carry on, knowing that the best of times is just around the corner.

Hope springs eternal in the person and work of Jesus Christ. Through His life, death, and resurrection, He bridged the gap between heaven and Earth. On the cross, He "disarmed principalities and powers" and "made a public spectacle of them, triumphing over them" (Colossians 2:15). He ascended to heaven to minister on our behalf and remains our hope—an anchor that "enters the Presence behind the veil" (Hebrews 6:19). No matter the challenges ahead, look to Jesus and rest in the assurance that the best is yet to come.

---

1. Jacques Doukhan, *Secrets of Daniel: Wisdom and Dreams of a Jewish Prince in Exile* (Hagerstown, MD: Review and Herald®, 2000), 162, 163.

2. Helmer Ringgren, "מַע and דֶּמַע," in *Theological Dictionary of the Old Testament*, ed. G. Johannes Botterweck, Helmer Ringgren, and Heinz-Josef Fabry (Grand Rapids, MI: Eerdmans, 2001), 11:179.

3. According to Jacques Doukhan, the following passages, among others, contain the verb with a warfare connotation: Joshua 21:44; 23:9; Judges 2:14; 1 Samuel 6:19, 20; 17:51; 2 Samuel 1:10; 2 Kings 10:4; Jeremiah 40:10. *Secrets of Daniel*, 183, 191n2.

4. Daniel 7:24 uses the Aramaic form of the semitic root *qûm* (rise, stand up), which in this context is a synonym of *'āmad*.

5. William H. Shea, *Daniel 7–12: Prophecies of the End Time*, Abundant Life Bible Amplifier (Nampa, ID: Pacific Press®, 1996), 214.

6. James Swanson, "רַשׂ (śăr)," in *A Dictionary of Biblical Languages With Semantic Domains: Hebrew* (Bellingham, WA: Logos, 1997).

7. Doukhan, *Secrets of Daniel*, 153.

8. Ringgren, "מִע and דַמָע," 11:179.

9. Alberto R. Treiyer, "The Priest-King Role of the Messiah," *Journal of the Adventist Theological Society* 7, no. 1 (1996): 64–78.

10. As noted by Francis D. Nichol, ed., *The Seventh-day Adventist Bible Commentary* (Washington, DC: Review and Herald®, 1977), 4:878, the book referred to here is the book of life (Daniel 7:10; cf. Philippians 4:3; Revelation 13:8; 20:15; 21:27; 22:19).

11. Ellen G. White, *The Great Controversy* (Mountain View, CA: Pacific Press®, 1950), 614.

12. Mitchell Loyd Chase, "Resurrection Hope in Daniel 12:2: An Exercise in Biblical Theology" (PhD diss., Southern Baptist Theological Seminary, 2013), 51; emphasis in the original.

13. *The Seventh-day Adventist Encyclopedia* (Hagerstown, MD: Review and Herald®, 1995), s.v. "Resurrection."

14. White, *The Great Controversy*, 637.

15. For the exegetical arguments in favor of the distinction between the partial resurrection mentioned in Daniel 12:2 and the general resurrection referred to in Daniel 12:13, see Artur A. Stele, "Resurrection in Daniel 12 and Its Contribution to the Theology of the Book of Daniel" (PhD diss., Andrews University, 1996).

16. Jacques Doukhan, "From Dust to Stars: The Vision of Resurrection(s) in Daniel 12,1–3 and Its Resonance in the Book of Daniel," in *Resurrection of the Dead: Biblical Traditions in Dialogue*, ed. Geert van Oyen and Tom Shepherd, Bibliotheca Ephemeridum Theologicarum Lovaniensium, vol. 249 (Leuven, Belgium: Peeters, 2012), 85–98. Indeed, to this article I owe the idea for the title of this chapter and the pattern for the other chapter titles of this companion book.

17. Ernest W. Marter, *Daniel's Philosophy of History* (Bracknell, UK: Newbold College, 1967), 115, quoted in Gerhard Pfandl, *Daniel: The Seer of Babylon* (Hagerstown, MD: Review and Herald®, 2004), 107. See also Le Roy Edwin Froom, *The Prophetic Faith of Our Fathers: The Historical Development of Prophetic Interpretation*, vol. 2 (Washington, DC: Review and Herald®, 1948), 528, 784; Le Roy Edwin Froom, *The Prophetic Faith of Our Fathers: The Historical Development of Prophetic Interpretation*, vol. 3 (Washington, DC: Review and Herald®, 1946), 270.

18. Nichol, *Seventh-day Adventist Bible Commentary*, 4:881.

19. Léon Levillain, "La Conversion et le Baptême de Clovis," *Revue d'histoire de l'Église de France* 21, no. 91 (1935): 161; author's translation. "La conversion de Clovis au catholicisme est un événement qui fait époque dans l'histoire du monde. Ses conséquences débordent, en effet, les limites du petit royaume franc sur lequel régnait le fils de Childéric à la fin du ve siècle et se font sentir à travers les siècles jusqu'à nous."

20. Elena Malaspina, "Clovis, King," in *Encyclopedia of Ancient Christianity*, ed.

Angelo Di Berardino (Downers Grove, IL: IVP Academic, 2014), 1:563.

21. Everett Ferguson, *Church History: From Christ to Pre-Reformation* (Grand Rapids, MI: Zondervan, 2005), 1:295.

22. Luce Pietri and Charles Munier, "Tours," in *Encyclopedia of Ancient Christianity*, ed. Angelo Di Berardino (Downers Grove, IL: IVP Academic, 2014), 3:814.

23. Jean Carlos Zukowski, *The Role and Status of the Catholic Church in the Church-State Relationship Within the Roman Empire From A.D. 306 to 814*, Adventist Theological Society Dissertation Series, vol. 10 (Berrien Springs, MI: Adventist Theological Society, 2013), 155.

24. Heinz Schaidinger, *Historical Confirmation of Prophetic Periods* (Austria: Bogenhofen Seminary, 2010), 33.

25. Shea, *Daniel 7–12*, 222, 223.